# We Just Want to Live Here

Amal Rifa'i and Odelia Ainbinder first met
during a student exchange trip to Switzerland in
the summer of 2000. They lost contact after the
Intifada broke out on September 29, 2000.
They exchanged the letters in this book from
August 2002 to November 2002.
They are now living in Jerusalem.

# We Just Want to Live Here

### A PALESTINIAN TEENAGER,
### AN ISRAELI TEENAGER—
### AN UNLIKELY FRIENDSHIP

Amal Rifa'i *and* Odelia Ainbinder
*with* Sylke Tempel

 ST. MARTIN'S GRIFFIN  ❧  NEW YORK

3 1257 01536 5652

Amal's name and other identifying characteristics have been changed to protect the safety of this Palestinian teenager and her family. The dates of the letters are in chronological order within each chapter, but they are not in chronological order throughout the book.

WE JUST WANT TO LIVE HERE. Copyright © 2003 by Amal Rifa'i and Odelia Ainbinder with Sylke Tempel. All rights reserved. Printed in the United States of America. No part of this book may be used or reproduced in any manner whatsoever without written permission except in the case of brief quotations embodied in critical articles or reviews. For information, address St. Martin's Press, 175 Fifth Avenue, New York, N.Y. 10010.

Maps: Peter Palm, Berlin/Germany

www.stmartins.com

Library of Congress Cataloging-in-Publication Data

Rifa'i, Amal.
    We just want to live here : a Palestinian teenager, an Israeli
teenager—an unlikely friendship / Amal Rifa'i and Odelia Ainbinder
with Sylke Tempel.
      p.   cm.
    ISBN 0-312-31894-4
    1. Ainbinder, Odelia—Correspondence.   2. Rifa'i, Amal—
Correspondence.   3. Arab–Israeli conflict.   4. Jewish teenagers—
Jerusalem—Correspondence.   5. Jewish teenagers—Jerusalem—
Attitudes.   6. Teenagers, Palestinian Arab—Jerusalem—Correspondence.
7. Teenagers, Palestinian Arab—Jerusalem—Attitudes.   8. Teenagers
and peace—Jerusalem.   9. Jerusalem—Ethnic relations.   I. Ainbinder,
Odelia.   II. Tempel, Sylke.   III. Title.

DS119.7.R497 2003
956.94'42'00835—dc21

2003046879

Originally published by Rowohlt Berlin Verlag in Germany as *Wir wollen beide hier leben*.

First U.S. Edition: September 2003

10  9  8  7  6  5  4  3  2  1

For my family, my husband, and my teacher. In memory of my late grandfather in Dubai.
—AMAL RIFA'I

For my family, friends, and the comrades from my Youth Movement, *HaShomer HaZair*.
—ODELIA AINBINDER

And for Moritz Tempel.
—SYLKE TEMPEL

# CONTENTS

## INTRODUCTION

I was feeling the fatigue of a longtime Middle East corre-
spondent. Between interviewing experts and politicians,
studying whole libraries on the history of the Arab-Israeli
conflict, doing research in Palestinian refugee camps and
Jewish settlements, I started to agree with what Solomon
wrote in the Bible thousands of years ago: "There is nothing
new under the sun." It has all been seen, it has all been
heard before . . .

Yet I still wanted to hear the voices of those in Israel and
Palestine who have to live in "that situation," who are formed
by it, and who will have to overcome it one day if they want
to live in peace with one another. I wanted to experience
and perhaps also demonstrate if it were possible, at least for
some younger people, to communicate with one another and
to find out about the possibilities, opportunities, and limits
of this endeavor. In that regard, Amal, a Palestinian teenager,
and Odelia, an Israeli teenager, fulfilled every expectation I
had. (This idea began, I must admit, as more of a hope than
an expectation for me.)

Two young women, who are only eighteen years old, have
taught me to throw overboard many things that I believed.

The openness of these young women, and their families, made it possible for me to delve more deeply into different world views than "I ever could have" been possible before. For me, they cured a disease that is very widespread among observers of and participants in the Israeli-Palestinian conflict: that is, to pass judgment too easily about "good" and "bad," to make the distinction too quickly between "victim" and "perpetrator," instead of first listening, remaining open to surprises, and accepting different perspectives—even though some might provoke objection.

Amal Rifa'i and Odelia Ainbinder are too young to remember the optimism engendered by the Oslo process and how the atmosphere had changed radically for the better, at least for a short time.

Euphoric Palestinians celebrated the return of their leader, Yassir Arafat. Incessantly, they raised their long-banned flags. Proudly, they commented on every new institution, which, of course, was even more proudly labeled "national." Very soon, many Israelis also believed it would be possible to live side by side with their Arab neighbors—without war, oppression, and terror. The debate continues as to what exactly caused the collapse of the peace process and what exactly triggered the outbreak of the Al-Aqsa Intifada in September 2000, in which more than two thousand people lost their lives.

This political debate is of minor relevance for Amal and Odelia. They, like so many their age and even younger, are the main victims. They grew up in a world where teenagers are killed simply because they went to a discothèque, met friends in a café, or took a bus to school. Where four-year-olds in Gaza or the West Bank know the exact meaning of the words *tank* and *curfew*. A world where youngsters are trained to believe that it is a holy deed to blow themselves up in a so-called "martyrdom operation" for the Palestinian cause.

Amal and Odelia were both born and raised in Jerusalem—but in totally different worlds. Even under normal circumstances, they probably would never have met. During the Six-Day War in June 1967, Israel conquered East Jerusalem, which up until then was governed by Jordan. In 1981 the Arab part of Jerusalem—which is called *Al-Kuds* by the Palestinians and claimed as the capital of a future Palestinian state—was annexed by the Israeli government. Arab inhabitants were "free to choose" whether they preferred to become Israeli citizens or keep their Jordanian citizenship and accept permanent resident status. Unlike Palestinians in the West Bank and Gaza, Arab residents of Jerusalem are entitled to National Insurance and invited to participate in the municipal administration. Most Arab Jerusalemites—like Amal's family—chose to keep their Jordanian passports and to boycott participation in municipal elections.

Even before the outbreak of the Al-Aqsa Intifada, contact between Israelis and Palestinians was limited. Only on Shabbat, when shops were closed in Jewish Jerusalem, would Israelis do some of their shopping in Arab neighborhoods. Arab Jerusalemites would, from time to time, eat out in (Jewish) West-Jerusalem restaurants.

Politics, however, is not the only factor that separates Amal and Odelia. Before the war of 1967, Amal's neighborhood was a small village at the edge of Jerusalem. Today it's part of the big city but still a very rural community. Its inhabitants basically belong to two or three big families. In her village, the old traditions are kept. For generations people have known each other and cared for each other. They meet for their weekly Friday prayers in the village mosque and take time for a little chat at the local grocery store. Together, they celebrate weddings, greet the newly born, or grieve over the dead.

Amal feels protected and secure in her world. It would not even occur to her to leave the safe familiarity of her community. In summer of 2002, she became engaged. To Odelia's surprise, Amal does not find it unusual at all to get married at the age of eighteen. Rather, she would consider it unthinkable to leave her parents' home and move into an apartment of her own, or together with other young people, let alone live together with her fiancée without benefit of marriage.

At the same time, Odelia decided to do a year of "community service" and to move into an apartment with friends from her socialist-Zionist youth organization *HaShomer HaZair*. Her life is not that different from the lives of many young people in the Western world. She listens to the same music, watches the same movies, knows the same sitcoms. After her year of social service, however, she will have to face a challenge young people in the United States and Europe do not have to face: She will do her two years of mandatory army service, which, writes Odelia—"poses so many questions about morals and integrity that kids like us are sometimes totally overwhelmed."

Under "normal" circumstances a young, married Palestinian and a young Israeli soldier would not meet. For many years or even decades, organizations like *Peace Now* or *Peace Child Israel* have tried to establish contact between young

Israelis and Palestinians. They were successful when both sides still believed in peace between these two peoples. When Israelis and Palestinians once again became entangled in the vicious circle of violence and retaliation, these non-governmental organizations (NGOs) encountered enormous difficulties, but continued to work with no less enthusiasm.

Amal and Odelia were introduced to me by *Peace Child Israel*'s Melisse Lewine-Boskovitch. Since 1988, *Peace Child Israel,* funded by private sponsors, has organized and still organizes theater projects in Israeli and Arab schools within Israel proper, but also with young Palestinians from the West Bank and Gaza. Both Amal's and Odelia's schools had participated in these theater projects and both girls were active in those projects—but not together. In the summer of 2000, a Swiss philanthropist invited those groups on a student exchange program to Switzerland. On this trip, Amal and Odelia met for the first time.

It was not the beginning of a beautiful friendship. Misunderstandings and the Israelis' lack of knowledge about Islam angered the Muslim teenagers. The Israeli group had invited them for an evening out in a discothèque where alcohol was served. This was viewed by the young Muslims as an insult to the traditions of Islam, which strictly forbids the consumption of alcohol. "The journey unfortunately started on the wrong foot," Odelia writes. But still she found it so much more interesting to make contact with the children from the Arab school than to stay with the "children of my own school whom I found rather boring." Both Amal and Odelia remember vividly how they also had "a lot of fun" playing ball games in mixed teams and giggling the night through when they shared a hotel room during a field trip in Switzerland. Despite the affection both girls felt for each other, the general distrust between the groups could not be overcome. In the end, the teenagers had spent many weeks together without establishing closer ties. Shortly after they returned home, the Al-Aqsa Intifada broke out on September 29, 2000. At that point, Amal and Odelia lost contact altogether.

For Odelia, the time before the Al-Aqsa Intifada seemed like a distant dream in which people did not live in constant fear of Palestinian suicide bombers. Now, Israelis avoided Arab-populated areas. Amal considered it impossible to keep in touch with her Israeli friends while at the same time seeing "so many of our people killed by the Israeli army." Only after some time had passed did she feel that she had "wronged a lot of my Israeli friends whom I have known from *Peace Child Israel*."

In June 2002, I began searching for a young Palestinian and a young Israeli who would be willing to share their thoughts in an exchange of letters. It is the young generation that suffers most from the violence both sides inflict on each other. Yet it is this same generation that has to take upon itself the task of finding a way out of this seemingly endless circle of violence. I hoped to find two open-minded young women who, at the same time, would represent their respective societies and be tolerant enough to listen respectfully to what the "other side" had to say.

The ongoing violence had almost destroyed the entire fabric of social relations between Arabs and Jews that existed before the outbreak of the Al-Aqsa Intifada. But an exchange of letters naturally requires some mutual trust. It was important, therefore, to find two people who knew each other and could at least look back on some positive common history.

I deliberately wanted to recruit two young people from Jerusalem for this book project. It is obvious that the political circumstances for Palestinians in East Jerusalem are somewhat easier than those in the West Bank or Gaza, whose inhabitants suffer from curfews and military actions by the Israeli army. At the same time, however, I wanted to portray the different cultural and political worlds in which Amal and Odelia were living. It was also important to me that both girls have a chance to meet. In contrast to Palestinians living in the West Bank and Gaza, East Jerusalemites are allowed to travel freely within Israel.

I met with Amal and Odelia separately at first. Odelia impressed me with her idealism, combined with a keen sense of justice. She can be very critical of her own society. At the same time, she is very deeply rooted in Israeli culture and very comfortable with her Israeli identity. Amal seemed to be much more torn emotionally. She tries to adjust to the reality "that the Israelis are the rulers," but, at the same time, feels deep anger about their occupation of Palestinian land. Amal was very skeptical about reestablishing contact with Odelia and the idea of exchanging letters with her. She had returned from her trip to Switzerland with the impression that all Israelis were unfriendly. Eventually—and with a little bit of mediation—both of them were able to clear up those misunderstandings.

Amal and Odelia chose the topics they wanted to write about themselves. The first letters are almost shy "protocols of thought." Both young women think about themselves and their future plans, but also wonder about the situation that the other one might be experiencing. We began working on this project during the summer of 2002, shortly after the end of their summer vacation. It was obvious, therefore, that they should write about their travel experiences—which could not have been more different. After that, both felt secure and courageous enough to dare to tackle more difficult topics, such as the outbreak of the Intifada. Their written words originated through Odelia's taped thoughts, letters to one another, and long conversations held with me and with each other. Since Odelia doesn't speak Arabic and Amal did not feel comfortable enough speaking Hebrew, we chose English as a "neutral" language. More and more, I became aware of a rift stemming from disparate views of the same history that deeply influences both of their societies.

With the beginning of the Lebanon War in 1982, and even more so with the first Intifada—the Palestinian uprising against the Israeli Occupation that began in December 1987—Israeli society became "individualized." Since Israel's creation in 1948, the common credo was: " 'We,' the Israelis are fighting for our lives, we defend our state against the enemies who want to destroy us." In the view of most Israelis, these wars—the War of Independence against six Arab armies, the preemptive Six-Day War (which broke out after a period of harsh rhetoric from and even more severe actions by then–Egyptian President Gamal Abdul Nasser), and the fight back against Syria's and Egypt's surprise attack on Yom Kippur 1973—were purely defensive and therefore morally justified. *"Ein Breira—There is no choice,"* was the slogan of those years.

The Lebanon War, as the Israeli Prime Minister Menachim Begin himself admitted at the time, did leave Israel a choice. For years, Palestine Liberation Organization (PLO) guerrillas had attacked northern Israel from their strongholds in South Lebanon. The Israeli government deliberately decided to end those attacks and in 1982 invaded Lebanon to destroy the PLO stronghold. In September 1982, a Christian-Lebanese militia committed a massacre in the Palestinian refugee camps of Sabra and Shatilla, near Beirut, under the willing indifference of the Israeli army. Deeply shocked, hundreds of thousands of Israelis protested against this war. Some soldiers and officers did the unthinkable: They dared to make an individual choice and refused to serve on the Lebanese front, despite the serious consequences—many of them had to serve prison terms. Some years later, many Israelis decided not to serve in the West Bank and Gaza, where they felt the government was suppressing what they considered to be a legitimate uprising against an occupying power.

For Odelia, it is almost natural today to have an individual choice. She and her friends discuss frequently "whether we should go to the army and change things from within or whether we should refuse" and become part of a slowly growing protest movement. Odelia decided to do her army service "because it is such a big thing in Israel and I want to know what it is like." Discussions between Odelia and her friends reflect the poles within Israeli society today—the need to serve a collective and the need to pursue one's individual happiness. This debate is very often expressed in popular culture. Political slogans on popular bumper stickers often make use of the word *"Am—The People."* *"HaAm rozeh Shalom—The People Demand Peace"* or *"HaAm im HaGolan—The People Will Not Return the Golan Heights,"* are two of the most widespread slogans. The well-known Israeli singer Shalom Hanoch mocks the use of *Am* as an expression for the collective: *"Al Tikra li Am"* he called one of his songs, which Odelia quotes. "Don't call me *people*. I do not want to be seen only as a part of a collective." In the third or fourth generation after the creation of the Jewish state, Israeli society—and Odelia for that matter—can afford a comparably high level of individual freedom.

Palestinian society does not yet know the luxury of an individual approach to history, since it is lacking the reassuring comfort of an independent national state. This society still perceives itself as a collective, sharing the experience of the struggle for independence and the end of occupation. Its collective narrative tells the story of the Palestinian dispossession, the loss of the Palestinian homeland, and the suffering under Occupation. There is little room for the personal, individual story. No wonder, then, that autobiographical Palestinian literature is virtually nonexistent.

Amal, of course, also tells us the collective narrative, since "just thinking that the Israelis took our land away and that hundreds of thousands of Palestinians became refugees still makes me angry," even though her family was spared the fate of the refugees. We also wanted to learn, however, about the perspective of this one young Palestinian girl. Many of Amal's letters originated in long conversations with me, prompted by many questions I asked about her and her family's history. It should be clearly understood that I did not try to influence her, nor to alter the style, the flow, or the content of her letters.

This book is about the perspectives of two young people who grew up amid a conflict they did not choose. In the

Middle East, people often confuse opinions with facts. The perception of truth is not necessarily the actual truth. It is because of those circumstances that Amal—and her parents—only agreed to participate in the writing of this book on condition that she would remain anonymous. Amal Rifa'i is a pseudonym. Amal's father especially, was convinced that a young Palestinian girl who would openly express her critical opinion about Israel would suffer dire consequences. Deeply concerned, he asked me during one of our first conversations: "What if she gets arrested for her critical attitude? What if somebody sees her leaving an Israeli police station and thinks she is a collaborator?"

His fears reveal the depth of distrust felt by a Palestinian family that tries to keep out of politics and—as much as possible—live a quiet life. Despite the father's reservations, Israeli security services would rarely bother to take an interest in the critical opinions of an eighteen-year-old Palestinian girl.

But it is also true that many Palestinians are made to work for and report to Israeli intelligence in the Occupied Territories. That may be because of the sad necessity for the Israelis to foil terrorist attacks. At the same time, this sows deep mistrust within Palestinian society. The results are often horrible. Somewhat arbitrarily, many innocent Palestinians are accused of being collaborators. Social isolation is one comparatively less troublesome consequence. Since the outbreak of the Intifada, more than one Palestinian has been sentenced to death for "collaboration with the enemy" by Palestinian tribunals. Some have even been lynched. It was essential, therefore, that we—the authors and St. Martin's Press—do our best to safeguard Amal's and her family's anonymity by changing certain identifying details about their lives.

Naturally, Amal and Odelia do not view the same historical events in the same light. Thus, a chronology about the conflict, and a glossary explaining the most important events, places, and religious terms, appear at the back of this book.

As we were writing this book, Israelis died in Palestinian suicide attacks and Palestinians were killed in military actions by the Israeli army. Curfews and closures in the Occupied Territories made life unbearable for the civilian Palestinian population. Amal and Odelia, as well as their families, were deeply affected emotionally by those events. To my great surprise, though, they were never really distracted by them. Whenever these two exceptional young women met, they turned into giggling teenagers in no time, cheerfully exchanging views about the most handsome soccer players at the 2002 World Cup Championship.

As difficult as it certainly was to tolerate or even accept one another's views, not for one moment did Amal and Odelia lose their warmhearted respect for each other or their open-mindedness regarding the other's perspective. That is so much more than both their leaderships were able to muster during the last years. *Shukran. Todah.* Thank you.

—SYLKE TEMPEL, Jerusalem, November 2002

# One

## TALKING ABOUT MYSELF, THINKING ABOUT THE OTHER

*Odelia*
*Jewish New Year, Kfar Saba, September 7, 2002*

Dear Amal,

I am sitting in my new room in Kfar Saba, a little town located some ten kilometers northeast of Tel Aviv. It's in the middle of the night and I am very tired but I am also very happy because this is the beginning of my new life. I finished school. I moved out of my parents' home in Jerusalem where I grew up and I am beginning a year of "community service." This is a voluntary year of doing social work before being drafted for the obligatory army service. My choice was to do community service in my youth movement *Shomer HaZair*. This is a socialist-Zionist youth movement that has existed in Israel and Europe and all over the world for ninety years already. Like most of these youth movements, it really doesn't play that big a role anymore in present-day Israel because youth movements are not cool, I suppose. You have to be an idealist to work for a youth movement. You have to think about your life, and the situation we are in. Most kids don't want to do that. They want instant answers. Like somebody who prefers to heat something up in a microwave instead of taking the effort to cook. Our youth movement is in bad shape. We haven't gotten a lot of kids who come to our activities; we have to work really hard on recruiting more.

This year I am going to be a *kommunar,* which means that I am in charge of a facility in Petach Tikva together with two other girls and a guy. We are responsible for the activities there and for the kids who look at us like "big bosses," turning to us when there's a problem. I am really excited that I chose to do that. I know it might sound somewhat strange and lots of people don't believe in it because it doesn't seem to be very realistic, but I believe in the chance that we can make the world a better place. In my youth movement, we want to teach the kids we are working with values like tolerance and freedom of thought. We want to motivate them not to look for easy answers.

*Shomer HaZair* owns an apartment in Kfar Saba for the people doing community service; fifteen of us will live on a commune. Of course, with a unique living situation we will have troubles and problems from time to time, but we will overcome them. We have already had long and often very intense discussions. It is so extraordinary that I am experiencing a socialist lifestyle, as in earlier days. During this year we have a shared economy and are supposed to share everything.

My long-term ambition is to become an actress. Actually, I am already an actress. I played leading roles in some performances staged by our school, but I want to become a professional actress. And when I say I am an actress, I mean one is born with the calling, in my opinion at least. That has nothing to do with what I am doing right now. My dream is just to be on stage every night, even if I might only get the minimum wage. I don't care. It is also my goal to become a well-known actress who reaches a wide audience.

What I wonder: Do you, Amal, have all of the opportunities I have or do you find it more difficult, because you are kind of a stranger in your own country?

Thinking about future plans involves the simple question: Do I have a future in this country? Or what is the future of this country? And I can't think of living somewhere else, at least not forever. Israel is my home. Which once again makes me think of you and how you feel about living in a place where you, at the same time, might feel so out of place in a country called Israel under a flag with the Star of David on it, which is a totally foreign symbol to you. I, of course, feel at home here. We practice my religion (I am Jewish). Hebrew is my language, and everybody around me speaks Hebrew. Would you feel better being in another place, or if you were living in a Palestinian state? I guess you would. How do you feel about this place? How would I feel if somebody took over Israel and told me: "OK, from now on this is a Christian country, we have changed the flag, our national symbol is the cross and the official language is—let's say— English." I guess that's what the Palestinians might feel. I wonder if you would prefer to stay here under such circumstances. Suppose the situation goes on forever—and I feel it might go on for some more years—perhaps you might go somewhere else?

I would like to go all over the world and live in other places, such as London. I always would come back and I always would feel at home here. Do you feel at home or do

مقتل ١٩ إسرائيلياً وإصابة ١٣٠ في عملية تفجيرية بنتانيا

Al Kuds, March 28, 2002
19 Israelis Killed, 130 Wounded by Bomb Explosion in Netanyah

you feel a little bit out of place? On the one hand it is, or it was, your land and your home, at least in my opinion. But it is definitely also my country, a country that has changed completely for you. We have a language spoken that is not yours and a flag foreign to you, even though you live only five minutes from where I grew up. Could you distance yourself from everything Israeli and ask: "Am I only a Palestinian?" But you would still live only five minutes from where I, an Israeli, grew up.

For the moment, I want to make this the best year of my life. I would love to conclude it with great results by recruiting lots of new kids into the movement to make it stronger, to learn how we can live together in a socialist way as much as possible. Then, to finish with my army service and hopefully to do something meaningful there, like participate in an educational program. There are language-training programs for Russian-speaking soldiers, for example. And then to travel as all Israelis do after the army. I would like to go to South America, come back to Israel, and try to get into one of the best acting schools, preferably in London or New York. New York sounds a bit too scary, too big, too American. I only "know" it from the movies and therefore I think of New York as a Hollywood cliché right out of *Batman*—a crime-ridden, capitalistic "Gotham City." But London sounds wonderful. I have been there twice already, alone, and it's really a great place. If neither school works out, I will just go to Tel Aviv and hopefully keep on living my life without having to think about whether I should take a stupid bus or not because I could die in a suicide attack.

I would love to live in a world where I would not have to answer my little six-year-old brother's questions about this political situation. I don't have the slightest clue how to answer him when he asks me, "Are all Arabs bad?" I tell him, "Well, Oded, our parents sent you to a mixed Arab-Jewish kindergarten, and now to a mixed Arab-Jewish school. Do you think that all the Arabs in your class are bad?" Thank God, my mother has to put up with my brother's questions most of the time. If I have kids one day—and I suppose I will, and I suppose the situation will not have changed much—I would not have the slightest idea about what to tell a six-year-old about *HaMatzav*—the situation.

This is my dream for the future. I want a normal life, not in the sense of "ordinary" with a nine-to-five job and a house in the suburbs. Of course, I want my life to be exciting, but not in a way that is "abnormal" or "too interesting" in this country. Not in the sense that today I was walking down the street and, oops, something blew up next to me. I definitely don't want my life to be "interesting" in that sense.

I guess that your plans for the future are different. I think you hope for a country for yourself. I don't know what I'd be doing in your place. If I were the same person but in your place, I might have the same dreams, but they would take on a whole different meaning. I suppose in Muslim culture no one encourages a young girl to go study in a foreign place like London. A more conservative, traditional family would probably consider a daughter with dreams like that to be rebellious.

I try to state my opinions because I think that is very important. And you should also try to state yours all the time, even if it is quite scary for us sometimes to hear what the "other side" thinks. If you say you don't have an opinion, you're a liar. If you don't state it, you're a coward. Recently, I came across a quote by Socrates that I really like: "The unexamined life is not worth living." I like the process of criticizing, examining one's life situation. To me, this process is a way of being sensitive to your surroundings, your environment. I also like just to approach life with this attitude: If bad things happen, well, then, I will deal with them, as I have to deal with the political situation we in the younger generation are thrown into. Writing this book means dealing with this situation. It is probably even some sort of therapy for me.

Odelia

*Amal*
*September 15, 2002*

Dear Odelia,

This might sound somewhat unusual: I have always dreamt about becoming a police investigator because I love to get to the bottom of things. That is, however, only a dream, which cannot come true. There are Arab police officers, Palestinians with Israeli citizenship who mainly live in northern Israel. But I am not a citizen, and it's not easy for an Arab girl to leave her home and live somewhere else where no-

מתאבד הרג 20 חוגגי ליל סדר במלון בנתניה; 4 בני משפחה נרצחו באלון מורה; שרון: ערפאת אחראי
24 נהרגו בפיגועי פסח; הממשלה התכנסה לאשר גיוס מילואים חלקי

Haaretz, March 29, 2002
Suicide Bomber Kills 20 Guests of a Seder Dinner at Hotel in Netanyah;
Four Family Members Killed in Elon Moreh; Sharon: Arafat Responsible
**Subhead:** 24 Killed in Attacks During Passover Holidays: Government
Session on Callup for Part of Reservists

body knows her, or where she doesn't have relatives.

I finished school with the Israeli *Bagrut* (high school diploma). Actually, this school is the only one that offers the option of an Israeli high school degree. (Arab students in East Jerusalem or the West Bank use the Jordanian school curriculum. Palestinians from Gaza follow the Egyptian curriculum.) I chose the *Bagrut* because that would prepare me better for a professional career in Israel; therefore, I traveled a long distance just to attend this school. With a Jordanian high school degree, I would have had trouble getting into an Israeli university because preference is given to students with an Israeli high school degree. If I wanted to study at an Arab university in either the West Bank or in an Arab country, I would have problems getting there because of the Intifada and the ongoing closures. Or I would have trouble finding a job afterwards. I know plenty of people who could hang their nicely framed school certificates on their living-room walls, but had to make a living from cleaning or working in the kitchen of an Israeli restaurant.

Even with the Israeli high school degree, it is not that easy to get into an Israeli university. You have to pass a very difficult psychometric test (intelligence and ability test). Only with good grades can you get into the really attractive departments like law or medicine. I was an excellent student at my school. But I couldn't score high enough on the psychometric test. Israeli kids are prepared for a whole year at their schools. At our school we could take an extra ten-day preparatory course that cost some 2,000 NIS (about $500 US). Ten days is just not long enough to earn high enough marks to get into the really attractive university departments. And our parents can't afford to pay for a special course as rigorous as the one the Israeli kids get. In our tradition, a family's father tries to build a house for his grown-up sons so they can marry, have a family, and move into their own home. A father of grown-up sons has to pay for their houses, or at least an apartment, for their weddings, which are really big celebrations, and for the education of all of his children—sons and daughters. How much else can a father shoulder?

I would have loved to study the law. I am a hard worker. I have lots of energy, and also, I am a fan of Ally McBeal on the TV show. She is clever and witty. But I am barred from attending the law faculty because of my low grades on the psychometric test. So my mother told me to study special education in an Israeli college here in Jerusalem, which a lot of Arab girls attend, meaning I will work with handicapped children. Well, I love children, and I have a lot of patience with them. With a college degree, I still might get into Hebrew University and pursue the profession I really want.

A few months ago, I met this friend of a friend at a wedding. I loved him at first glance. He is kind, intelligent, and has a really good character. In July, he proposed to me, meaning that he came to our house and told my father that he wanted to marry me. I did not intend to marry early, nor did my father intend this for me. He always told me to get a good education first. But, according to our traditions, we marry soon after we get engaged. Besides, we want to avoid gossip. Officially, our neighborhood is part of the big city of Jerusalem. But it is rather like a little village. Most of the people there belong to two or three big clans. They all know each other, and they care about what the others are doing.

My daddy will pay for my studies even though I will be married and my education is not really his responsibility anymore. But I will also work to pay for the tuition, which is some 12,000 NIS a year (about $3,000 U.S.) and my husband will support me. He had dreamt about studying, but then he also wanted to build a home for himself. Being married will mean a lot of new responsibilities for me.

I had thought about studying somewhere else—in Jordan, for example—and getting away from our little village for a while. My father would have liked me to study in Jordan; we have relatives there. But my mother insisted that I stay here because I would have a better chance of getting a job. And now I cannot leave my fiancé behind, anyway. Living in a place other than your hometown isn't that easy. I am also wary of new things. I even hate to go to downtown East Jerusalem. The boys constantly harass you—"Give me your telephone number" here, "Hey, Darling, you're beautiful" there. No young guy would dare do this in our village. People are very conservative; they would beat the guts out of anyone who didn't show sufficient respect to somebody's daughter or sister. Nobody ever harassed me in Bethlehem or Ramallah, or in other places under Palestinian Authority. The

Palestinian police would not allow it. They probably would give those guys serious trouble. Sometimes, however, the people in our village keep their eyes open a bit too much.

I also want to have an exciting life. I want to do something that gives my life meaning. Should I decide to live in this country, then I certainly will not move away from my village. But my fiancé and I thought about living somewhere abroad, at least for some time. He wanted to become a journalist or writer, but he didn't do well on the psychometric test either. At the moment, he earns money as a construction worker. He gives me a lot of books to read; he himself reads Arabic and Hebrew fluently. I often read his writing. I like his stuff very much; he is bright and has good ideas. But I am afraid he is losing his ambitions, all the dreams he once had. I don't want this to happen to me. But there are so many restrictions and regulations.

Sometimes I compare our situation to that of the Israelis. I see them running around with their guns; I see their nice neighborhoods, with those clean playgrounds and well-paved streets. They are so privileged.

My brother visited some of the Palestinian refugee camps—even before the Intifada when it was easier to get into those places. The kids showed him their paintings: Mainly, they painted guns. This is their reality. They hardly ever see Israeli civilians, only soldiers with guns. They grabbed stones and then told him, "We don't have guns like the Israelis, but we have stones and we want to throw them at the Israeli occupiers." This is how they grow up, and what they think of even when they are still very young. They don't play with dolls or cars; they don't think of their studies. They want to become fighters when they're older. They don't have a future.

Often I am very jealous of the Israelis. They have so many more opportunities; they are richer and can send their children to universities or even abroad. I cannot live like them. Everywhere I look, there are restrictions. It is as if somebody told me, "This is your place. Don't leave it." Nobody tells the Israelis what to do.

This is my land, but not my country. Like everybody else among my family and friends, I try to ignore the Israeli reality around me. If I didn't, I would feel as if it were choking me. We don't speak about politics outside our home. My father is afraid that he could get arrested for it. He is our only breadwinner. Who would then take care of our family? You see what happened to Marwan Bargouthy, the Fatah leader in the West Bank: He said the plain truth and now he sits in an Israeli jail. I admire him a lot. Speaking my own mind is not so easy. My father tells me to shut up. He is worried because he knows that I have a furious temper and a big mouth. He knows that I have trouble seeing everything that's going on around me, and not speaking out. But it is dangerous. I don't even talk to my friends about politics.

So I just try to live my own life and control my temper. Like this one time at a supermarket when an Israeli girl waiting in a line behind me said to me, "Why do you smile so stupidly, you stupid Arab?" I would have liked to hit her, but this certainly would not have been a good idea in a supermarket in Jewish Jerusalem among a crowd of Israelis. So I just kept on smiling, which made her even angrier. But I can't control myself forever. I respect my father so much and he understands this situation better than me. But I would not accept it if a soldier at a checkpoint told me that I could not pass. I would sit there and wait until they finally let me in, instead of allowing them to send me back home. I am too lively and confrontational a person.

I hope for equality. I would like all the differences to disappear completely—Arab, Jewish, whatever. Yes, this is my land, and I don't want anybody in it to tell me what to do.

Amal

*Odelia*
*October 1, 2002*

Dear Amal,

I wish I were there at that supermarket when that stupid Israeli girl harassed you. Because I would have hit her, and nobody could have done anything to me except think that I was totally out of my mind. I guess that's a privilege we Israelis have. You would get in trouble; I only would be called crazy, and I couldn't care less. I have heard this kind of harassment so many times. I hear people make nasty remarks about Arabs on the bus, standing in line somewhere, and, God, it is so frustrating. It makes me so mad. I feel like shouting at them. So, I really understand you. But it is good you kept on smiling at her, even though you were furious, because she saw that you were not hanging your head and letting her frustrate you. That's really admirable. I believe that people want to get a reaction out of you when they do this; they want to start an argument. Same as these people who want a war all the time—they want to provoke and get a reaction. So what I try to do is this: I try to give them a really smart answer, smile at them, and walk away. When I hear people make those slanderous remarks, I sometimes shout at them, sometimes say something smart, and then just get off the bus.

You are not happy about how difficult it is to pass the psychometric test and get into university. I don't know whether you know this: We have the same difficulties. We don't get it for free. People came to our school and offered us a course for about 2,000 NIS ($500 U.S.). We also have to take this course and take the test. Israeli Jews don't necessarily get good grades on the test. I, for instance, don't want to take the psychometric test, which will cost my parents some 2,000 NIS ($500 U.S.) and give me some score that seals my future. I want to get into acting school, and I do not need this really stupid test to apply to acting school.

Moreover, Israelis are not always happy and live in big houses as you might believe. I do not live in a big house with a nice garden at all. My father doesn't earn that much. We are doing OK, but we are certainly not rich. And, just like you, we are also not allowed to go into the Occupied Territories, we are also banned from going to Bethlehem or Ramallah. It is not as if anybody tells the Israelis what to do. If the army closes those areas, they are closed for everybody. And many Israelis don't get jobs. You can have a *Bagrut* [high school diploma], get high scores on the psychometric test, and a degree in whatever subject, but you might not get a job because of all of the unemployment out there. I don't know whether you have noticed this, but Israel as a whole is in bad economic shape, so right now, apart from your religion or passport, everybody is having trouble.

Israelis who go to university pay a hell of a lot of money

for their education, only to be unemployed after graduation. That's something that also happens in a lot of other countries around the world—everybody nowadays has problems getting a job with a college degree. It is true that Arabs are more discriminated against and have more difficulty getting into universities or getting jobs—especially now, after the beginning of this "Intifada." But I can assure you: I hate those tests, and I am going to have a hard time taking the psychometric test. I know that I will get a bad grade and that's why I have not taken it yet. I still have a whole year of community service and then two years of army service and besides—I really want to go to acting school. And I really hope that I will get in. I want to try acting and if that doesn't work, I will take the test, study something not as exciting, and get a regular job. But right now, I am eighteen and I have the right to be idealistic and dream about a grand future.

I do not agree with what you wrote about Marwan Bargouthy. He is not sitting in jail because he was just telling the truth. He was arrested because he is suspected of having ordered terrorist attacks against Israeli civilians. Perhaps some people do get arrested because they are "just speaking their minds." But that's certainly not the case with Marwan Bargouthy.

To me, it's also a really strange thought that you are getting married at such a young age. But I see that you want to keep on studying and get a job and that's cool. You are not stopping your life because you are getting married, which is nice. With some people it's just their goal to get married and that's it. You are not like that, and that's good. What is also funny to me is that people would gossip, or that you probably are not allowed, according to your tradition, to visit your fiancé at home. Those differences between our cultures are amazing to me. We have more of a Western culture, and in a Western culture you are supposed to be alone with your fiancé and spend time with him. I guess I won't get married for a long time—if I get married at all. And if there were somebody, I would first want to live with him. After all, you have to know how he behaves—how you get along with him!

I hope you are happy because you sound happy. I'm glad you sent me pictures of you and him. He looks handsome. Congratulations.
Odelia

*Amal*
*October 5, 2002*

Dear Odelia,
We are a conservative family that respects tradition and religion as a whole. Therefore, in our religion it's not permissible for a man or a boy to go out with a girl or for a girl to sleep in the house of a boy she doesn't know—this is why you see girls marry at the young age of eighteen. Why? So that they don't sin or what we call desecrate the family honor. That's why the girl gets married to the boy she loves, because she cannot have a relationship with him except after getting married. My family is understanding. My father gives me freedom to choose, if a man asks for my hand. But there are families that disregard the girl's opinion because they consider her to be too weak to make her own decision. I think that is wrong.

I like my religion so much. The Islamic faith truly respects a person, it requires people to respect other people, and therefore I respect myself. I am not required to wear a head-scarf, which I also don't do, at least for now. But I am not allowed, for example, to wear a short dress, shorts, or shirts without sleeves. Because my body is for myself, and not for other people to look at. I don't envy Israeli girls who wear those tight clothes. I don't have anything against marrying early. You could be engaged, but still you are entitled to break off the engagement if you do not want to marry the man. I would not like to live with somebody before marrying. I don't like the idea of having a relationship with somebody before marrying him. I respect my tradition and religion. It makes me feel safe and secure.

My parents always want the best for me. They want me to have a good education, and also a happy married life and this is the reason that they help me as much as they can with my education. For us it's hard to get into university, espe-cially because I want to get into Hebrew University. The tuition is very high and I also have to become fluent in He-brew. And on top of that, I have to get really high marks.

There is something else: I think it is somewhat strange for you to tell me that you Israelis are also not allowed to go to Ramallah or Bethlehem. That's certainly not the same thing; your situation is completely different. Going to Ramallah or Bethlehem doesn't mean as much to you as it does to me. All your life you did not go to those places before this Inti-fada and—as you told me then—you went to Bethlehem the first time when we made the trip there together with the exchange group from Switzerland. That's the difference: Ra-mallah or Bethlehem are Arabic, not Israeli. This has some meaning for me, not for you. I am not allowed to visit a place that is really *my* country, the land that is to become the Palestinian, not the Israeli state.

I also totally disagree with what you said about Marwan Bargouthy. I strongly feel that he was speaking his mind, and that was why he was arrested. Look at me! I am speaking my mind, but I prefer to remain anonymous; I hide my identity. He does not hide his identity and that is why he is in jail. He is not a spy. He is not a collaborator. That's why I think that he is a good person and a good leader.

There are many people in Palestinian society who are collaborators, who work for the *Shin Bet,* the Israeli Secret Service, and inform on people. Like when such people tell them where to find some activist who then is killed by the Israeli army. Very often these people are tempted by money because of their very bad economic situation.

I first heard about Marwan Bargouthy when he began to appear frequently on TV at the beginning of the Intifada. I admired him because I thought that he was telling the truth: that we don't want to be occupied anymore and that we have to fight in order to get what belongs to us. And he was not afraid to tell the truth in front of everybody. I like that. I think it is absolutely wrong to put him in jail.

Yours,

Amal


P.S. My Jewish friends in *Peace Child Israel* told me that they took preparatory courses for a whole year for the psychometric test—for free. And the teacher who gave us the extra course confirmed that as well.

*Odelia*
*October 12, 2002*

Dear Amal,

Sorry for insisting on that: This girl from *Peace Child Israel* must have been at a very expensive, exclusive school in Israel. Through my youth movement, I know a lot of people from different parts of Israel. None of them were offered a free course for the psychometric test at their school. They all had to pay for it.

I don't think we can agree on Marwan Bargouthy. I don't believe that he was arrested because he "spoke the plain truth," as you say. He isn't a journalist or a writer. He was the leader of the *Tanzim,* which is affiliated with Yassir Arafat's Fatah movement, and which has perpetrated many attacks against Israeli civilians. That's why he is standing trial.

You say that you would never sleep at a boy's house if you didn't know the boy. Neither would I. Why would I sleep over at the house of somebody I don't even know? But sleeping in a friend's house doesn't mean anything. I mean, my girlfriends had lots of sleepovers at each other's houses and that was a lot of fun. Even when I had a boyfriend and went to sleep over at his house, it didn't necessarily mean that we slept with each other. I mean, we also know our limits. We know what to do and what not to do. And when I say that I would like to live with a person first, it also means that he would be a "long-term boyfriend." None of us moves in with somebody just like that.

Yours,
Odelia

*Amal*
*October 25, 2002*

Dear Odelia,
I guess there is a misunderstanding here: I am not talking about sleeping in a girl's house. I sleep in my girlfriends' houses all the time. But I am certainly not allowed to sleep in a boyfriend's house without being married to him.

I don't think that we can reach an understanding about the psychometric test. My friend certainly was not from a rich school, and from what I know, their teachers trained the students during regular class how to best answer those questions.
Amal

# Two

## MEETING THE OTHER IN SWITZERLAND

*Odelia,*
*Jerusalem, August 25, 2002*

Dear Amal,
The idea of meeting and sharing a trip together with a Swiss exchange group and the Arabs was, at first, really appealing—just to get to know people with totally different views and ideas. The Swiss were older than we were, eighteen, nineteen, but it did not make a difference. If they had joined eighteen-year-old Israelis, the difference would have been stronger. Israelis at that age think about the army and what they will be doing in the next two or three years. The Swiss guys were so relaxed; it was a relief. They talked about the things they wanted to study, the traveling they were planning. I immediately had the feeling that Switzerland was so free and rich, so free of our troubles.

The problem was, though, that we didn't have enough meetings with the Arabs beforehand; we didn't know them that well. So the problem had already started when we just invited them to go downtown with us to have a drink, or to go to a discothèque. They always declined our invitations, always kept to themselves, and we really didn't understand why. They always came up with excuses. We took them to one of the places we liked, some argument started, and when I came back from the bathroom, they had all disappeared, saying the place was too filthy, and that they shouldn't drink anyway. So we said: OK, next time we'll know, but somehow the trip had started on the wrong foot. Except for my friend and I, who really liked to be with the Arabs, there was no interaction between the Arabs and the Israelis. My friend and I were the exception because we didn't like the other kids from our school; we liked the Arab kids better. Besides, when you meet new people, you don't have enough time to hate one another.

In Switzerland it was different, because we were simply enthusiastic about being abroad, doing all the tourist stuff. It was thrilling to see snow on the mountains in August. Back home, the whole group had another program: We visited all the holy sites—Christian, Muslim, Jewish. That was before this Intifada started, and we really didn't talk much about politics.

Only once, when we were at Masada, did I address Arab-Israeli politics. There they had audiotapes for almost every language in the world, except Arabic. I was furious; I thought that made us just a racist society. And I said so in English for everyone to hear, which our Israeli guide did not like. He told me, "Don't say that in front of our guests," which made me even more furious. Later, when I calmed down, I understood that I should not have said that. Masada is such a Jewish symbol, and very, very rarely, if ever, visited by Arabs. So, why should we have Arabic audiotapes then?

Visiting Masada was funny: The guide spoke about the

meaning of the place. That the Jews who resisted against the Roman oppressors would rather commit suicide than be defeated and sold into slavery. Most of us Israelis, just fifteen years old, thought that was pretty stupid. It was pretty difficult to understand the seriousness of this, when we were only fifteen years old.

Before Switzerland, we were just thinking about the fun we would have traveling around in a group and going abroad. There were tensions between us and the Arabs because we were not very well prepared. We left the Swiss guys in the role of mediators, trying to calm things down, and really felt bad about it because they were friends with us and the Arabs. Often the Arabs felt misunderstood; they felt that their traditions were not sufficiently respected. No one had prepared us not to ask them out for a drink or to go to a discothèque. We didn't know how different we were. We thought they were like us. Young and happy to spend some good time with each other. But now, it would be even more difficult. Things have changed. Both sides are much more extreme and nationalistic because of the Intifada. And we are different because we have now seen more, witnessed the beginning of the Intifada, and become more political.

Yours,
Odelia


*Amal*
*September 10, 2002*


Dear Odelia,
Just like you, I also was thrilled to go to a place with a beautiful landscape like Switzerland and, as I learned during

الرئيس بخير وموجود في مكتبه وسط جنوده ومقاتليه

رام الله تحت الحصار واقتحام مقر الرئاسة وسقوط ٥ شهداء

Al Kuds, March 31, 2002
President Unharmed; Holds Out with His Fighters and Soldiers
**Subhead:** Ramallah Under Siege; Army Invades President's Palace; Five Martyrs Killed

this trip, these were such nice and friendly people for hosting a group of Arab and Jewish kids.

You say that there was a misunderstanding from the beginning and that our two groups—with different ideas, lifestyles, and religions—did not know each other too well before the trip. I was not there, but I heard about the incident when the Jewish group invited some of the Arabic kids for an evening out at discothèques and in bars. But I was told that the Arabic kids really were angry, and that they were insulted that the Jewish kids had asked them out for a drink, and taken them to places their religion forbids them to enter. I do not want to blame the Israeli kids entirely for it, because I think the adults should have prepared everyone. But how come they didn't know about the customs of a people they have lived next to for the last fifty years? How come they didn't know we are forbidden to drink alcohol? The Arab kids were so angry, they didn't believe that the Jewish kids would not know, and thought it was done on purpose.

There were different kinds of troubles in Switzerland as well. It was decided that we would make trips to some of the neighboring countries, including Germany. I was excited.

פיגועי ההתאבדות בירושלים, בתך אביב ובבקה אל-גרבייה; פלשתיעאי רצח שני אזרחים בנצרים
מצור על לשכת ערפאת; 7 ישראלים נהרגו בסוף השבוע

Haaretz, March 31, 2002
Suicide Attacks in Jerusalem, Tel Aviv and Baka al Jarabiya; Palestinians Kill Two
Civilians in Netzarim
**Subhead:** Arafat's Headquarters Under Siege; Seven Israelis Killed During
Weekend

One of my brothers had been there on a school trip and he
was enthusiastic about the place. People were so nice and
kind, he said. His host parents treated him with so much
love that their own son got a bit jealous. But the evening
before our planned trip to Germany, when we had gathered
for a dinner together, one of the teachers came to our table.
There's a problem with the Jewish group, he said. One of
them does not want to go. He says that he had lost family
in the Holocaust and would by no means set foot on German
soil.

We Arabs were mad; I was especially furious. What is this?
Only because some great-great grandparent was killed, he
does not want to go? What's his problem? My brother told
me that the Germans were nice and friendly and this young
kid does not even want to talk to them? And who is discriminated against by whom? We Palestinians by the Israelis. I
wanted to see the place myself. I wanted to get back home
and tell my brother that I'd been there, too. And this was
spoiled. I wish the Jews would forget. It would perhaps make
them a happier people.

But I don't forget that we had fun times on the trip as

well. There was the party an Arab friend threw on the roof of his house where we all listened to Arabic music and even though not everyone came, still Arabs, Jews, and the Swiss were dancing together. We played ball games in Switzerland, forming mixed teams—and we were great at overcoming all of the problems there were between us. I also remember the trip we made to the Swiss countryside, and you and another Jewish girl shared a room with me and another Arab girl. I respect you because I could feel that there were no reservations on your side, no hatred or bad feelings. At least not in front of me. Unfortunately, the trip wasn't long enough for us to really become good friends.

Well, I enjoyed the trip, and at the same time, I was confused by it. Arabs and Christians have different lifestyles but yet, the Swiss respected our customs. They did not take us to places we could not go to, they did not feed us food we could not eat. And, of course, they were so friendly to us. My host parents were wonderful; I felt like a daughter to them.

A few weeks after we came back the Intifada began. Looking back, I am not so sure if this wasn't a political maneuver to take Arabs and Jews on that trip. Perhaps the Israelis wanted to present their best side. I doubt that I would like to go on such a trip again now.
Amal

*Odelia*
*September 16, 2002*

Dear Amal,
I don't think that we took this trip to Switzerland, because the Israelis wanted to present themselves as good people.

Israel has involved itself with many student exchange trips over the last few years. I think that sometimes people should not always look for a cynical reason for what is going on. The idea of having a student exchange of a group of Arab- and Jewish-Israeli students together is terrific. Why do you think the idea was inspired by propagandistic reasons? The trip happened before the Intifada began.

I still think the problem was the lack of preparation for the trip. We knew that we would meet Arabs, but we didn't have the slightest idea about how to act. I know it might seem stupid that we didn't know much about their religion and so on. But the guides and other people who were in charge of the project just didn't tell us anything. We didn't get to know each other before we went to Switzerland.

Also, I think this country needs to change its approach to education. Why do we have to take a test in English, but we don't have to take a test in Arabic? Why do we learn about what happened in I-don't-know-where and we don't learn anything about the culture of the people living right next to us?

In all my years in Israeli high school I never learned anything about Arab traditions, history, or Islam. Perhaps my classmates learned some stuff in the seventh grade, when Arabic is taught. I wouldn't know; I was living in the States at the time. And I would very much love to know more about it.

This is where we were coming from. We just thought about having fun and meeting new people; we did not think for one minute about showing disrespect for the Arabs' different customs. I am sorry if we hurt your feelings, but it was not on purpose. I really doubt that the purpose of the delegation was to prove that we are good people. I think that it sprang from good intentions. Our trip was not organized by *Peace Child Israel.* The idea came from a Swiss lady, who gives a lot of money to different organizations which are active in promoting Israeli-Palestinian understanding— among them *Peace Child Israel.* It was an outsider's idea: Let's get people together. Obviously, we did not really know how to go about it.

I don't know if you remember that I was pretty angry about our lack of acknowledgment of Arab culture throughout the trip; I argued with the Israeli guides, and the people who came with us. When we were at Masada and there were no audiotapes in Arabic, I shouted at people that they were racist, and the Israelis told me not to say this in front of the foreigners, and I yelled back, "Yes, sure. Let's ignore reality."

But I also remember that we had a good time. My friend Tal was with you and your friend Samira; we had fun. We can overcome these tensions.

When our guides asked us how trip was and what we would change, we told them that it was a problem that we didn't know you before, how you live, and what your customs are. I really think that we should enact some major changes in this country and that Arabic should be taken much more seriously as a second language. My younger brother goes to a two-language school. The Arab kids come from an Arab neighborhood, the Jewish kids from all over Jerusalem, and he is learning Arabic as a second language. I envy him because he can write his name in Arabic, he can say Arab words, and he sings songs in Arabic. I don't have all this knowledge and I think it's a big loss. I don't even know the

Arabic alphabet, because I was in the States when Israeli students my age were studying the language. My brother is going to be seven soon. He speaks Hebrew with the Arab kids, and they speak Arabic with him, and they understand each other. That's what should happen.

It is really complicated at my brother's school, because they have to try to keep most of the Muslim, Christian, and Jewish holidays. My little brother learns about Islam, Christianity, and Arab culture—not only about Judaism and Jewish history. My parents worked hard to get him into that school because they hoped that this would bring about some change. So I am happy that my brother will have a much better connection with children of a different background and maybe when he is on a student exchange program, he will know how to behave better. He won't have communication problems, and he will never consider inviting his Muslim friends to a bar.

I hope they open more schools like that. I hope that people in this country will understand that they don't live in Europe or in America. We live in the Middle East, surrounded by Arab countries, and we should at least know what people are talking about all around us.

In the end, I had an interesting experience on this trip. I was more frustrated by the Swiss. I felt neglected by the girl who hosted me; she just simply ignored me. Switzerland was nice. It was beautiful; and all of it—the fun and the misunderstandings—was a learning experience.

I hope that there will be more Arab-Israeli exchange trips in the future. I also hope that the students will be better prepared, and that the kids will know what to do, and what not to do, perhaps putting nationality and identity aside for a while and remembering that they are just human beings, teenagers who love playing basketball. They could all become friends, and only later on discuss all this Israeli-Arab, Muslim-Jewish, whatever conflict.

This summer, I went to summer school in England, where lots of young people from different parts of the world came together. I was part of a mixed Arab-Jewish group from Israel. In the beginning, I didn't understand why the Arabs in my group, who were Israeli citizens, wanted to call themselves Palestinians. Now I understand this better, their need for a Palestinian state, and a Palestinian identity, even for Arabs with Israeli citizenship. Now I get it. Now I know how important it is to have a Palestinian state, and I am for it, I am completely for it, although I don't like all those boundaries either . . .

Now I have a much better understanding of how difficult it is even for those Arabs who do not live in the Occupied Territories, but are Israeli citizens, to live in a Jewish country when they are not Jewish. That's a big problem. But most people in this country, and even on the outside do not understand and perhaps do not want to understand. I don't know why. I don't know why people want conflict and war. Really, I sometimes feel as if they want war all the time. People do not really want to sit down for a second and think, yes, right, this is what the Palestinians want: Why can't we give it to them? Let's stop playing games. I hope that the Palestinian state will come into being. I don't know whether it will happen soon because people are strongly against it. But I really hope that you will get a Palestinian state soon. I really hope you will feel better and feel connected to some place, and I hope you won't have all of those stupid problems

at airports and borders. Gosh, I really hate that. I just hope
that you will get what you want one day.

There is another thing I would just like to add: You were
very angry about the one Jewish guy who did not want to go
to Germany. Well, I happen to know that today he himself
thinks that it was pretty stupid of him not to go. But you
can't just ignore the Holocaust and say that you "wish the
Jews would forget because perhaps it would make them a
happier people." Come on! If forgetting makes people happier, than why won't the Palestinians forget what has been
done to them so that they can feel happier? In my opinion,
it is not about remembering and wanting revenge, but remembering and trying to learn from the past. Forgetting the
Holocaust wouldn't do any good. Besides: It is impossible
anyway.
Odelia

*Amal*
*September 22, 2002*

Dear Odelia,
I feel that there is a very important difference: The persecution of the Jews in Germany and in Europe is over. The
Holocaust happened fifty years ago. Now, you have your own
state and everything, and still the Holocaust is not forgotten.
But our conflict is not over. We do not yet have a state; we
still can't live in peace and quiet in our own land. If, one
day, we have what you have—our own state, equality, jobs—
then, we will forget everything. Because the Arabs are known
for being forgiving. Besides, if we were not willing to try to

forget, then why would we even start those peace talks with the Israelis?

I also don't mean that *you* went to Switzerland for political reasons. *You* are different from most Israelis, anyway. There are few with your high morals. I thought it was a political trip because of the places we visited while we were in Switzerland. There was this politician in Bern who spoke to us. My Swiss host told me that in the original itinerary for the trip there was no place for the Arabs to visit; we were visiting synagogues and Christian places, but no Muslim sites. Only after she intervened did we also visit two mosques and speak to a Muslim from Pakistan when we visited Geneva. Only then did the Arabs in our group have the feeling that we and our culture were respected sufficiently. And that it wasn't only Israelis who got recognition. So how could I not think that it was a political trip?

Yours,

Amal

*Odelia*
*September 30, 2002*

Dear Amal,

What do you mean by "You are different than most Israelis, anyway?" That's such a generalization. I am not different than most Israelis. There are many Israelis who think the way I do. And how would I have come to my conclusions? I have a family who supports my views, friends, and the people from my movement, *Shomer HaZair.* It might not be a majority of the people, but still there are many who think the way I do. And even then, we are not one "group." My friends might have the same ideas in many respects, but still come to some different conclusions, because the situation is s-o-o-o complicated. All Israelis are different from each other; we are not *one*. I don't feel as if I am one with people. We are human beings with different ideas and thoughts that in some cases are similar. Sometimes we disagree, and we have plenty of political arguments. My friends and I have many discussions and arguments about how we would like to make the world a better place and what's right or wrong. Also, in my movement we argue and discuss a lot of issues. What I try to do is not pretend that I have the one and only truth, but rather try to see the whole picture. And to get this way of thinking across to the kids we work with as well. We try to be as objective as possible. I say to the kids: "Yes, our movement stands for a certain opinion. I have my own ideas, but so should you." In our work with the kids, we try to help them become critical-thinking adults; we want to encourage them to think for themselves. Most Israelis are like this.

I also think it is very odd when you say "There are few with my high morals." There are not just a few with what you call my "morals." Really. If there were only a few with "my morals" in this world, I would not want to keep living in it.

I also don't really think one can compare those two things— the Holocaust and our conflict with the Palestinian people. To me, the main difference is: For more than fifty years our two nations have been fighting a war over land. It was fought many times (not between an army and unarmed civilians) but rather between Arab armies and the Israeli army, like in 1948, 1967, and in 1973. What happened in Germany was totally different. There was never a war between the Jews and the Germans. Jews did not want any "war" with Germany. Indeed, they were and wanted to be considered equal citizens of Germany. I am sure that there are unfortunately many massacres or mass killings in the world. But I also believe that the Holocaust was unique. Never before and never again was a mass murder so efficiently organized, so "well prepared" in advance by discriminatory laws. And committed in camps, which only served to kill millions of people.

Here we have a fight over land, which we can solve once there is a peace agreement. The Jews of Europe were killed only because of a racist ideology and anti-Semitism. This is why I think that the Holocaust should not—and cannot—be forgotten, even if we badly wanted to forget.

I am not always sure that I like the lessons we drew from that part of our history. My friends and I were discussing this a lot after our history classes at school. We did not like the fact that some people in our own society came to the conclusion that we should feel compelled to fight all the time, and that we constantly have to defend ourselves. We could not understand why, after a suicide attack, some people would scream, "Death to Arabs!" That, to me, is pure racism, and not self-defense. It was obvious to my friends and me that we should fight all forms of racism, no matter what the source. Violence, in all forms, is absolutely unacceptable and no solution to anything—ever.

As an Israeli, I am familiar with the horrible situation here after the Intifada began. I am very critical of our behavior. But I wonder how many of our critics abroad would act if they had to be constantly afraid of suicide attacks. I know what it is like to live in a situation like that. But still I wish that people could overcome their fears and their anger and would understand that only an agreement with the Palestinians will bring us some peace and quiet. It is difficult to ask that understanding from people, who saw their loved ones killed. And that is what outsiders don't seem to understand. We are all human and our behavior in this conflict sometimes is only too human; and hard to overcome.

I still don't believe that it was a political trip only because we spoke with some politician in Switzerland. Besides, we visited the Swiss parliament and this politician only explained to us what was going on there. Actually, I remember it being rather boring. We didn't even talk about politics at all. Not with him, and not during the whole trip. The fact that a Muslim site was not put in was stupid, once again. People probably just didn't think carefully.

Yours,
Odelia

*Amal*
*October 4, 2002*

Dear Odelia,
I did not say that you were the only open-minded person in Israel. But still, people who think the way you do are in the minority, obviously. There are some 5 million Israelis, and certainly the majority do not think the way you do. Because if they did, perhaps the situation would not be like this.
Amal

# Three

*Odelia*
*October 1, 2002*

Dear Amal,
It never occurred to me that I could visit the West Bank or
Gaza. Regardless, my parents would have worried about me
too much. With the Switzerland group, we visited Bethlehem. After all, there were Arab kids in the group. But this,
of course, was before the Intifada. It was a cool place, like
the Sinai without the sea. Even though it is only ten minutes
by car from where I live, it is different there. It was like
going to a different country. Everything was cheaper, and
we spoke English because the Arab kids told us to speak
English in order not to be identified as Israelis. "Just in case,"
they said. I wanted to go there again, but there was no
chance to because the Intifada started.

Now I see the place on television and think: Wow, it looks
so different from when we saw it. Back then, there were lots
of tourists. And now there are tanks. When we were there,
everybody in the group spoke about going back there for
Christmas to the Church of the Nativity, because that would

be a chance to go to a Christmas service finally. I have never been to one in my life before. From the Jerusalem neighborhood I grew up in, I can see the Christmas fireworks in Bethlehem. I saw on TV all the lights and the decorations and the celebrations, and my friends and I really wanted to go there so badly. Now I sometimes drive by the street that leads to Bethlehem. The only things you see are an Israeli checkpoint, roadblocks, and certainly no tourist buses.

On the one hand, I understand your wanting a state, wanting the recognition of your Palestinian identity. Then I think: Why couldn't we just forget about being Palestinian and Israeli and live together? There are all these cultural differences, but it could be like in America, with their Chinatowns and Little Italys and whatever they have. The problem here starts with our wanting to be a Jewish state and giving everybody a problem who isn't Jewish. I know this is what we really wanted to be, but we achieved it. We have a state and yet we still keep on fighting and fighting. If there were peace, we could all be sitting in Bethlehem having a cup of coffee. It would be so cool if we could just cross over there as if it were the Sinai. You get a stamp in your passport, nobody harasses you, and you are in a different country. And it would be the other way around—you would come to our side.

Now we have war again. I don't really remember anymore how it all started, but I remember that my mother and I wanted to go to the Old City to buy shoes because they have nice, cheap shoes there. We didn't go that Saturday because the day before, there were demonstrations on the Temple Mount or the Haram al-Sharif. OK, we thought, it's going to be over soon; let's go next week. We didn't the following week, or the week after. Ever since then we have not gone to the Old City at all. I remember the beginning of the Intifada as the time when my mother and I didn't buy shoes.

Like everybody else, I thought it would be over soon, despite all the incidents we see here so often—the shootings and demonstrations, and police everywhere. We all thought that we would go to the Sinai over Sukkot in the fall of this year. It usually feels natural to go to the Egyptian Sinai for a vacation. Everybody cancelled; everybody was worried. Nobody went, there were no Israeli tourists in the Sinai over Sukkot. Then I understood that it would not be over soon. And that a new routine had begun. You would be checked everywhere, whenever you wanted to go out in Jerusalem or any other city in Israel. We wouldn't go out anymore. We were scared.

Now there are thousands of soldiers everywhere, we are still getting checked at every café, discothèque, or bar we want to go to. But we have gotten used to it. The other day I went to the pedestrian zone in Jerusalem. Just like before the Intifada, there were, lots of young people, music playing, fun things. And I thought: What, no suicide bombers here today? You get cynical, you start using black humor in order to cope with the situation. Today there was a small bombing in Jerusalem. "Small" is when only a few people get hurt and nobody gets killed. We were kidding about it: This bomber wasn't worth anything. Didn't kill anybody. This is what the situation does to you.

You try to tell yourself: Let's at least pretend this is a normal country. Let's at least try to have a normal life and hold on to our ideals and the thought that you have a future in this country. Because, really, I love my country, even though I am very critical of many things here. But I was

الجيش الإسرائيلي يعتقل مروان البرغوثي؛
صدور أمر توقيف بحقه كذريعة لمحاكمته

Al Kuds, April 16, 2002
Israeli Army Arrests Marwan Bargouthy; Warrant Published as Pretext for Trial

born here. I love the shared language—this is the only place
in the whole world where Hebrew is spoken as the primary
language. Hebrew is my mother tongue and the language in
the books I read. Every country has its own character. I like
the Israeli mind-set. Israelis are especially friendly and help-
ful. Total strangers will strike up conversations on the bus,
and if an Israeli has been hurt on the street, people will
immediately rush to see if they can help. There seems to be
a very strong bond between Israelis that extends beyond our
country. Whenever Israelis meet in other countries, they in-
stantly connect.

Are we different from others because the situation here is
different? I don't like to think that. Perhaps the Palestinians
feel different, since they can't go where they would like to
go; for example, to study in Tel Aviv. Personally, I don't feel
different from any other young person. I see the same films,
listen to the same music, watch the same TV shows. But,
yes, the situation makes me feel different, perhaps act different, causes me to feel more worried about my life. But
aren't wars happening everywhere in the world? Didn't they
happen in other places before they happened here? And isn't
racism something you find in lots of places? I feel kind of

רה"מ: ישראל תיסוג מג'נין בעוד יומיים, ומשכם בתוך שבוע
ברגותי נעצר ברמאללה; שרון: הוא יועמד לדין

Haaretz, April 16, 2002
Prime Minister: Army Will Withdraw from Jenin Within Two Days; Within One
Week from Nablus
**Subhead:** Bargouthy Arrested in Ramallah; Sharon: He Will Face Trial

special right now because news channels all over the world
are constantly focused on us. It is as if everybody is talking
about me and my country all the time.

It is really strange. Here we have all this progress—the
Internet and high tech for which Israel is really well
known—but at the same time we are stagnant because this
war has been going on for such a long time. The army is
cooler now, it's high tech, meaning that we can kill people
more efficiently. But it is as if we were stuck forever. Sometimes I feel really tired and try not to think about it. We
Israelis like this sort of escapism. We always try to escape
and pretend to have a normal life.

But of course nothing is normal when things happen like
the number 32 bus bombing some months ago. I could hear
the explosion. It was the bus that basically took all the kids
to my school. The whole school was in a panic. There was
supposed to be a Bagrut (high school diploma) exam this day
and they postponed it. All kids and teachers frantically
started calling their friends' mobile phones. The same thing
happens after every attack: You immediately try to call your
friends to check whether they are all right. Today I got a

phone call from my parents who were checking on me because close to the pedestrian mall there was an attack. I was at home, turned on the TV, and saw that there were only wounded victims. No special news on TV, no special music on radio, like when many people die, so after two minutes I also went back to what I was doing before: planning a birthday party for a friend.

And even after the "big ones," you talk about it with your friends, then you feel fed up about the whole thing, you say to yourself, Nobody I know died, and you try to go back to your daily routine. You feel scared often, you look around yourself on a bus and I have gotten off more than once because some guy looked suspicious. And I feel horrible, because I am afraid and because I have to be suspicious of people only because they look Arabic. The last thing I want to be is a racist. But in a moment where you really feel scared, you don't think about feeling "intolerant." You fear for your life.

I wish so much that things were different. That we could just go over there to the Arabs and they could come over here. I go to demonstrations. I am active doing all sorts of things, but I don't see how all those demonstrations really will change things. And every day I hope that none of my family or my friends die, and I try to have a life. Perhaps I should leave the country for a while and get a break. But I know that wherever I went I would switch on the news to see what happened at home. Perhaps we need a miracle.

Yours,
Odelia

*Amal*
*October 3, 2002*

Dear Odelia,

Yes, shortly after we came back from Switzerland, the Intifada began. In Arabic we use the word *Intifada* for "getting rid of a very bad government," meaning a government that does its best to control the people, to kill randomly, or to order the destruction of the people's belongings. *Intifada* means that one does not have a choice but to free oneself from that regime.

Let me remind you that the Intifada started because Ariel Sharon went to the Haram al-Sharif, knowing that by doing that, he would destroy all prospects of peace with the Palestinians. He didn't care a bit about the holiness of the place to all Muslims and that this act would utterly provoke the Muslims. The real reasons for this Intifada are the lack of respect for a Muslim holy site he showed with his visit and the suffering of the Arabs in their own homeland. And, really, the Palestinian people suffer up to this very day. Yet, still they hold on like no other people because they want to be treated equally. What they have gotten so far is nothing but beatings, jailings, and being killed. Only to achieve the simple things of equality and freedom. Those people who got killed left behind families, parents, wives, children. Who takes care of them now?

I also remember Bethlehem, the place where you and I spent such a lovely time in one of the cafés. Bethlehem has become a miserable place. The café where we were doesn't exist anymore. Buildings have been destroyed. People are now homeless; sometimes up to fifteen people have to share one room. There is no work in the Palestinian areas, so they try to get jobs in Israel. But time and again they are turned back by Israeli soldiers. So I really cannot blame them if they feel that they would rather blow themselves up than just wait to die of starvation. I believe that the Israeli government is responsible for this because it obviously wants to see a lot of Palestinian blood.

We have contact with Israelis. My father had lots of Israeli-Jewish business partners whom we would see sometimes at their houses, and sometimes they would come to our house. We would pay them a visit when they were sick. We had Israeli neighbors around the corner. Sometimes I thought: How can that be? Some of them are killing our children. They swear at my father, but at the same time, there are those people he likes enough to bring to our house.

My father has told us one thing: not to judge people as all the same, not collectively. That there were good Arabs and bad Arabs as well as good and bad Israelis. And that if you treated somebody respectfully, he'd treat you respectfully. On the one hand, every Palestinian has some fury in his heart, but then on the other, I think this situation was forced on us. We, especially those of us who are young, did not have a choice, so most of us try to make the best of it.

With the beginning of the second Intifada, I felt really bad. I didn't go out. I would sit in our living room and watch the news all the time. I became more furious by the minute. How could they do this to us? How could they kill so many of us—children and grown-ups? At that point, I felt as if I did not want to have anything to do with the Israelis and that each and every Palestinian should be in the streets fighting them with all their might. I only thought of Israelis as oppressors then. During the first six months of the Intifada, I felt a lot of fury and hate, and did not know how to express it. At that time, I discarded the whole idea that people would be nice to you if you'd just be nice to them.

Now I feel that I have wronged a lot of people by feeling that way and withdrawing completely from them. At times, when I was not watching the news on TV, I would sit down and remember certain times three years ago. I remembered my Jewish friends and how I was nice to them and how they were nice to me. And those memories made me feel very conflicted. Did I want to fight for my people or return to the past, to what I had before when I was friends with some Israelis? I still feel very confused about it, but I don't feel that terribly painful conflict within me that strongly anymore.

God gave people minds to think with, and I believe that we should use them. Instead of using their God-given minds to think with, Palestinian people would celebrate when they saw dead Israelis and Israelis would be happy when they saw dead Palestinians. Seeing all these deaths on the daily news, I reached a point when I just could not take it anymore. I came home from school and asked my parents: How many people were killed today? The same question the next day, and the day after that, and so on. I couldn't bear it any longer. I was exhausted, almost bored by it; I knew I could not deal with it any longer. I felt helpless. And this is the reason my mind told me to back off, to withdraw. Deep inside, however, my feelings have not changed. I feel, like each and every Palestinian, this huge rage like a flame inside me. I have the feeling that my dreams are dead or buried. How could I ever be able to do what I want to do with this situation going on? Could somebody please tell me when all of this will be finished, over, done with?????

Like you, I cannot visit the places anymore where we had spent some time together. I have friends and family in Gaza, Ramallah, and other villages I cannot visit—and they cannot visit each other. I live in my own homeland like a stranger. I want to be free like other human beings, without this distinction between "Jewish" and "Arab" and, most of all, without discrimination. I don't want to see bloodshed every day, as if to confirm the saying: "Man is born in pain but he dies quickly."

I wish it were more like America here, where people from different ethnic/religious communities coexist, but the Israeli government never leaves anybody alone. And if the Palestinians did not fight for what belongs to them, the Israelis would just take everything. As is happening right now.

In order for you and me to stay friends, I try not to imagine that one day you could be in the army and you or one of your friends would stand in front of me and keep me from going to Jerusalem to pray, or to Bethlehem or Ramallah to visit some friends or family. What would you do? Would you let me in, thanks to our friendship, or would you do your job and obey your orders?

I hope you understand,
Amal

*Odelia*
*October 10, 2002*

Dear Amal,
Actually, there are some things about America that suck. My family and I lived in California for two years and I could not

really connect to the people there. I thought that many of my classmates were very shallow. We have really important problems in Israel, while in California the biggest problem seemed to be whether to go to a shopping mall or a fitness center. But what I liked about America is that different ethnic and religious groups can live with one another. I still think that it would have been nice if we were living in this kind of society. I mean, if we hadn't come and taken this land and conquered it by war. It would have been nice if we could have put our identities behind us and could have called ourselves, I don't know, blablas and live in blabla land. I am, of course, aware that that is not possible.

As I said: I am for a Palestinian state and I think you should fight for your rights in a nonviolent way, because I am totally against violence.

When I showed my mom those letters, she was a bit angry about your justifying those suicide bombings by saying: Why should they not bomb themselves instead of dying from starvation? But I agree with you completely; I understand what's behind your words. They don't have much to lose. They live in destroyed houses. What can they do? I see that they are starving, frustrated, and sad, and constantly fed slogans urging them to kill Israelis. But still I don't understand why they would keep on doing this. Nothing is getting resolved by it; we all have to stop fighting and start listening. And when you teach your kids that violence is heroic, then nothing will ever change. I am not only talking about Palestinian boys or girls who are told that it is honorable to kill Israelis. But also about Israeli society, where many kids are taught that the army is the best thing, that one should always look up to the army, and that it is a great thing to be a fighter, to kill lots of people—"bad people," of course. Only in the last couple of years have we slowly stopped glorifying the army that much. Most of the parents in Israel don't like the idea of sending their kids into the army too much anymore because they fear for their lives and are tired of this war.

I understand that if you don't have a place to live and anything to eat and nothing to look forward to and you're helpless then, yeah, why not bomb yourself and take some Israelis with you? But I don't understand why some Palestinians keep on educating their kids to become martyrs. I just wish people would change their ideas completely. My family is trying to make us understand that the world is not black and white, and that in our conflict, nobody is only a "victim" or a "perpetrator." This is why I didn't like the approach of the Bush administration after September 11, when the president said in his speech: "Either you are for us or you are against us" and divided the world clearly into "good guys" and "bad guys." I also don't like that Muslims in general were perceived as the "Enemy." The world is full of people from different cultures and we have to understand each other as much as we can. I don't know whether kids in the Palestinian schools are taught about tolerance, about acceptance. Those students should not be taught to fight all the time or even that it is wonderful to become a *shaheed* (martyr). They should understand that this a complicated conflict, a complicated situation, and that it is not black and white. Perhaps that would lead to nonviolent efforts to reach an understanding. But I do see the difficulty in that they see violence around them all the time. For me it's easier to educate my little brother because he does not see violence on the street, as many Palestinian children do. But when we

both have a state, we will start living together, because these
are geographically such small places. There is no way to escape our living together.

I think it's good to dream about different people sharing
equal rights: Look at Martin Luther King. He was a true
hero. I admire him; too bad he's dead. People with opinions
like his all seem to get killed. There is a poster of Albert
Einstein hanging on the wall of our *kommuna* in Kfar Saba.
It says "Great minds always encountered violent opposition
from mediocre minds."

Martin Luther King was a black man in America fighting for
black people's rights. Black people were discriminated against
by law in the American South. They got mugged, raped, and
lynched just because of the color of their skin. Martin Luther
King always maintained his commitment to nonviolence. He
always preached not to go in that direction, not to become a
violent person. It's not going to help you win your rights. I saw
a movie about him, and in one scene, his house gets demol-
ished. People come with their shovels and pitch forks and
scream, "We will take revenge. We will show those who did it
what we are made of!" And he stands there after he barely
saved his kids from the house. "No, we are not going to be violent," he says. "We are not that kind of people, and we will
not get anywhere by using violence." You only provoke a violent reaction. At that time there was segregation; in the buses
he had to sit in the back because he was black. There were
benches and even public toilets for "colored" or for whites
only. Just to call them *colored* people or even worse words like
*niggers* was such an insult. And this man was above it because
he was smart and knew that success in the political arena
would not come from violence.

Violent opposition will bring nothing but a violent reaction. That's how I see it, too. We have been fighting the same war for more than fifty years and we are now in "the situation" that has been going on for two years. And it's not going to stop, because this stupid Sharon government comes up with all these stupid ideas and the most stupid one of all is resorting to violence. Many Palestinians might think: The only way we can get a state is by force, so let's blow up a bus or whatever. And, of course, they get a violent reaction back by the Israel government. That's the way it works here in the Middle East. When somebody hits you, you hit back. That's not how it should be. If you want to live a happy life, if you want to wake up with a smile on your face and not have to worry about getting killed, then it definitely would be better never to resort to violence. Sure, there's always a chance of getting killed if a piano falls on you from the fifth floor. But refusing to respond to violence with even more violence would at least make the chances slimmer of your getting killed on a bus or by a bullet.

I think we should look at great people like Martin Luther King and try to learn from them. I am not that surprised that he was killed. Why wouldn't people kill him—what he practiced did not correspond with how the world works. People should try to stop running after power and money all the time, trying to be the biggest, the strongest, and the best. Yes, in order to pursue the dreams you have, you also have to be very strong. But it doesn't make sense to pursue money and power so that you can look down on or oppress other people. We should try to think for ourselves, be individuals rather than following the crowd displaying all these nice pretty posters and spouting all these catchphrases like "We are one people. We are strong. Only together will we win." Oh, come on. You wanna win, go ahead, do it. But "Don't call me a nation."

That's a line by the singer Shalom Hanoch—. *Al Tikr'a li Am*. I don't want to be *Am*—"the people." I don't want to be part of this collective. I want to try to change things. I know it's not going to work because I know the world doesn't want to listen. At least, I have a book to put my views in and perhaps a few people are willing to listen and it will change their minds.

I would like to conclude with a song by an Israeli rap artist named Muki. Like all rap artists, he criticizes society. Translated, he sings about the following: "It's not a mistake, my brother, this is reality—a whole world filled with anger and loneliness. Look, there is so much stupidity, brother, there is nothing simple but everybody wants it fast and easy. Only himself can man change and see that the world has changed. There are so many doors that we will never open. How will we wake up in the morning if in our heart there is a hole? I don't see the light. Sisters and brothers, this is the time to get up and to live. We can't sleep anymore and want to make it happen, because if you haven't learned it by now, maybe you'll never learn. How many years have we got left? No one wants to be alone. A person is just a person. What is between blood and blood when you divide the world into 'us' and 'them' into 'for us' and 'against them'? The earth is weeping. The earth is crying." I think he makes his point.

Yours,
Odelia

*Amal*
*October 13, 2002*

Dear Odelia,

My daddy also taught us that there are bad people and good people on each side. But then, my family does not live in such a horrible situation. We don't live like those people in Gaza or Nablus who don't have anything. In front of their eyes, people get killed, children get orphaned, or lose brothers and sisters. So the parents have to explain that.

I remember the first time I felt that I was different, and that life was not always happy for us—it was when I was about eight years old. It was the time of the first Intifada, which basically went into its fifth year. People in East Jerusalem were very active in this Intifada; it was less "quiet" in Jerusalem then than it is during this Intifada. Not only the Palestinians in the refugee camps, but also the people in East Jerusalem were fighting the Israeli soldiers in the streets. There were clashes every day—even though it was not so dangerous in our neighborhood. My father kept us pretty much away from the demonstrations. But slowly I started to realize more clearly what I was seeing every evening on TV, all these episodes of violence. We did our shopping very often in Israeli stores. And very often I heard people say nasty things; I heard them swearing at us. I didn't understand the meaning of those words, even though, interestingly enough, all the bad words in Hebrew are Arabic and they throw them right back at us. Their hatred was directed against Daddy, and I felt very hurt that these people would insult my father. It was about this time that I asked my father to buy me a big sword so that I could defend him against people who wanted to humiliate him. I also remember that, one day, I took all the stones I could find in our garden up to my room and lined them up at the window—if Israeli soldiers came, I would throw my "munitions" at them. I wanted to fight like the children I saw on TV. I saw on TV how girls my age fought against the Israeli soldiers, and I saw how many of them got wounded or even killed. I asked Daddy what that was all about. I asked whether I would also be killed and carried away like the kids I saw, on a stretcher, or in somebody's arms, covered with blood. At first, he graciously lied at me. "Chabibdi, my Darling," he said, "it's only a movie. It's not real life." But everybody in my school talked about it, and one day one of the students got killed. Each and every one of us came to the funeral and sat for some time with his family. That's also customary in our tradition. So I confronted my father. I wanted to really know what it's all about. He told me: The Israelis have taken the Palestinians' land and the Palestinians are fighting to get it back.

Perhaps some of the parents who have young children during this Intifada also lie to them. But there will be a time when they understand, because they see what is going on with their own eyes. They will see fighting and tanks and Israeli soldiers searching their homes at night, and they will understand. Perhaps those parents also want their children to learn something else, but how can they teach them another way with all that is going on around them? Those children keep on drawing tanks and helicopters because it is the reality they see. They are not drawing the stuff of their

dreams and pictures of what they would love to become. They are drawing their reality.
Amal

*Odelia*
*October 17, 2002*

Dear Amal,
You were saying that the Intifada started because Ariel Sharon visited the Haram al-Sharif, or Temple Mount, "knowing that by doing that he would destroy all prospects of peace with the Palestinians." I totally disagree with that. I dislike Ariel Sharon from the bottom of my heart; in his whole career he thought things could only be solved by force. He had most of the Jewish settlements in the Occupied Territories built. I disagree with everything he is doing and I don't like him as my prime minister. But the problems in the Occupied Territories cannot only be blamed on the Israeli government. The Palestinian Authority wasn't doing much either to make the lives of the people in their areas better. They didn't create jobs for them or anything, and contributed a lot to their frustration. Therefore, I don't think only the Israeli government or Ariel Sharon visiting the Haram al-Sharif were responsible for the outbreak of the Intifada.

What happens in the Territories is horrible. We totally agree on that. But Arafat is also pretty much of an idiot. He doesn't know how to build a country, and it is dreadful to think what would happen to those poor people, who are already very poor, under a leadership like that once there is a state.

To me, there is also a difference between Arabs in the West Bank or Gaza and Arab Israeli citizens. If you are a citizen, you can ask for your rights in your country; you can even go to court. I accept that Arab Israeli citizens would not consider the same things "holy" that we do. But they probably would not want to move to a Palestinian state because they are used to living in Israel and because this is their home. What they are asking for is to be treated as equal citizens. It's a different story with the Palestinians in the Territories. Arabs inside Israel want equality. Palestinians in the West Bank and Gaza want a state. That's a huge difference. So we have two different wars. One for a state that is very violent. And one that is nonviolent, because it is about citizens' rights. The struggle for citizen's rights is waged not only between Arabs and Jews, but also between Jews who came from Europe and those who came from Arab countries, between newcomers like the Russians and Israelis who have lived here for a much longer time, between rich and poor.

I even think that most Israelis agree that there should be a Palestinian state. They know that it will happen anyway. If not now, then in a few years from now. What I think is: Having a Palestinian state would give you, Amal, a place where you would belong. But if your neighborhood in Jerusalem would not become part of that state, you still would stay in it because it's your home, right?

You are so right when you say that the situation was forced on us. But I think you are wrong when you say that we don't have a choice. I think we *do* have a choice. We can make a change. We are the next leaders of our world. I am sure this is a great responsibility, and we have to decide now what we want to do with our lives, whether we will sit down and just wait to see what happens or whether we want to take responsibility for making positive change. "The leaders of tomorrow" sounds so much like a stupid slogan. But it's true that things will be in our hands. Stating our opinions will also make a big difference, because that way we can show how we want to shape our future.

You know, once again it is easy to blame the Israelis for just about everything when you talk about people starving. Yet it is not that easy. There are lots of human rights organizations in Israel that provide food and help for the Palestinians. My movement sends packages of food to the Territories. There are lots of Israelis who try to help because they are very unhappy with the situation.

Very often civilians are killed. But most of the time the army tries not to kill civilians but to focus on the terrorists. Mistakes happen all the time and killing in general is terrible. But all in all, they try to spare civilians.

Terrible things also happen to Israelis. If we were occupied by the Palestinians, I am not sure there would be the same situation. We remember, for example, things like the lynching in Ramallah, when right after the beginning of the Intifada in October 2000 two Israelis were arrested by Palestinians because they had lost their way in the Occupied Territories and were brought to a police station in Ramallah. A mob stormed it and they just lynched them in front of everybody and people were watching and cheering, and the police did nothing. Except to say afterward that what happened was regrettable.

I admit that sometimes I have my doubts that Israel is still a democratic country. Yet the other day I saw a documentary about an incident that took place in the mid-1980s. A public bus was kidnapped by Palestinian terrorists. Eventually, it was stormed by Israeli security forces. The terrorists were caught alive, but mysteriously at some point later, they were found dead. Even some officers were suspected of having killed them, and the whole affair was covered up for a while. But at last the officers were put on trial.

Those people clearly were terrorists who were about to blow up a whole busload of people. And yet the officers were finally sentenced for having killed them, even though one could say that this is exactly the security forces' job. I was impressed when I watched this documentary. By putting these officers on trial and by showing this documentary, the judicial system in Israel was sending a message: Even if they were terrorists, the moment they were caught and disarmed, nobody had the right to kill them, and, therefore, the officers were guilty of a crime. The fact that they had to stand trial and were found guilty gave me the feeling that we still try to behave as morally and as democratically as possible. Would there be a trial in the Palestinian territories, let's say against the ones responsible for the lynching of two Israeli civilians in Ramallah? I doubt that very much.

I believe that Israel is very often judged according to much higher standards because it is a democracy. But I also think that it is wrong that authoritarian states like most of the Arab countries very often are not judged according to the same standards, even when those regimes commit human-rights violations.

I think we should always remember that two sides are fighting this Intifada. Even though there is a difference be-tween me and you, Amal, on one side, and the people who live in the Occupied Territories, because they have to suffer most of the violence. And still, we both could get hurt by this war because there are also lots of Arabs, Israeli Arabs, who live here, who are killed in those suicide attacks. There is no winner in this war, Amal. Only losers.

Yours,
Odelia

*Amal*
*October 25, 2002*

Dear Odelia,

You are saying that the Palestinian leadership also is responsible for lots of the frustration because they did not create any jobs. Where would the Palestinians get all these jobs? There are so many Palestinians who studied and have good qualifications and they still don't have jobs, because the economy in the Palestinian Territories is very bad and there is no real infrastructure for highly qualified people. I still think the main reason for the outbreak of the Intifada was that Ariel Sharon went to the Haram al-Sharif. This place is so holy to us. Sharon just wanted to show that he was the big boss and that he could go wherever he wanted without paying respect to anybody.

I know that in the Palestinian leadership there were all these problems with corruption. I have my own thoughts about our leadership. Yassir Arafat never dared to act against the Israelis. He couldn't do anything without their OK. Probably not even go to the bathroom. This is also what drove people mad. Finally, when Yassir Arafat went to Camp David in the summer of 2000, he understood that he had to do something about it, that he had to show his people that he wasn't doing whatever the Israelis and Americans told him to do. This is why he said "No" to what was proposed there.

The Palestinians were happy because he had told them that, like Salaheddin, [Sultan of Egypt and Syria who conquered Jerusalem—or liberated Jerusalem from crusader rule—in 1187 A.D.], Arafat would get Jerusalem back. At Camp David he refused to do what the Americans and the Israelis asked him to do because he would not have gotten back Jerusalem. Besides, Yassir Arafat is our only real leader. Who would come after him?

Now the Palestinians cannot stop the Intifada, because every day there is more destruction and more people are killed and so on. But I also know why people keep on fighting. In our religion, the faith in an afterlife is deeply rooted. If your earthly life is really miserable, if you are constantly told what to do, then you would rather fight until you are free and die, if necessary. You would not be afraid because Allah would take care of you and guide you. See, for us Muslims, it is absolutely unbearable to be told what to do and to be checked constantly by people who are not from our own faith and tradition. And, above all, from people we think stole our land. I know that sometimes in other Arab countries people are not really free. But at least they live among their own.

It also tortures me that so many people get killed. I agree with what you think about the lynching in Ramallah. I think it is totally against Islam. When you are talking about the army trying to remain moral, you should also not forget: We don't have all these modern weapons like the Israeli army, the F-16s and Apache helicopters. And every so often,

Palestinians get killed by Jewish settlers or the army and
there is hardly an investigation against them. Every so often,
I have said that I also would rather have a happy life, and
not get involved. But I truly think that if the Israelis would
stop, then we would stop. If they would give us Jerusalem,
we would stop. I definitely want the Haram al-Sharif to be
under Arab Muslim rule and I don't want any Israelis there.
Yours,
Amal

*Odelia*
*November 3, 2002*

Dear Amal,
I was a bit frustrated when I read your last letter. I tried to
explain so many things, to show a different point of view
among Israelis. That it is not only us doing all the bad things,
as it is perceived abroad most of the time. And that instead
of thinking who has done whom wrong, I, like many Israelis,
would rather come to an understanding. After all, I believe
that is also in our interest.

I don't really like to get into political arguments. That's
something for the politicians who could sit down and pull
out their maps and discuss how exactly things should be
done. Only recently I started learning many things about
politics, or the history of our conflict. And I am definitely
not familiar with what exactly happened at Camp David. I
know there is a big debate in Israel about it—my parents
also have their arguments about whether it was perhaps only
96 or even 97 percent of the West Bank to be returned to
the Palestinians.

But I know one thing for sure: If we really think that we have to keep on fighting only because we have fought so much already, then I would say, OK, that finishes every chance for a dialogue between Israelis and Palestinians. It's a dead-end road. It's not logical at all to say that because so many people got killed already, we cannot give up the fight, and then some more people are killed.

Really, I have to quote Martin Luther King again. You know what makes really good leadership to me? The bravery to resist your own people if it is for the sake of their future well-being. Martin Luther King did not accept violent means just because many of his people wanted it. And he succeeded with his nonviolent resistance and, in the end, his people revered him for that. I think it does not make sense to say that Yassir Arafat had to say "No" in Camp David because his people expected that from him. Or that he "never could do anything without Israeli approval." After all, the PLO had fought against the very existence of Israel for so many years. He certainly did not need Israeli approval for that. I think that, after the Oslo accords, both sides should have been motivated to get something done together, instead of fighting each other, and to try to make positive things happen, to build something for the future. As far as I know, the Palestinian leadership got a lot of money from the United States and Europe to build a state, and they really failed badly.

If we wait for the other side to stop fighting, we probably will never stop. That's what I try to support in my society and that's what I think should perhaps also happen in the Palestinian society. I think it is so much more important to be smart than to fight all the time. To me, it would have been smart not to pay attention to whether Arafat's people wanted him to say "No" but rather to look to the future and try to get a better deal. See, I just think it makes a lot more sense to build something in this world—even if it is not quite perfect—than to fight, be killed, and get absolute justice and rewards in the next.

Yours,

Odelia

# Four

TRAVEL

*Odelia*
*August 25, 2002*

Dear Amal,
I love to travel around the world. The first time I was sitting on a plane was when my family and I were on our way to the States to live there for two years. My father, a computer specialist, had a new job in Silicon Valley. I was twelve then.

When I was fifteen I went to Croatia with a friend who had family there and it was lovely. At the age of sixteen I was in Switzerland with our group. The past two years I was in England twice—last year in London with my friends. We had a lot of fun, feeling really independent. This summer I went to the International Summer School in Wales. Except for the time I traveled with my parents to America, I always traveled on my own or with friends.

But if you ask me what's my favorite place in the world, it's right here in Israel: the mountains of Eilat. It's gorgeous; it is the most beautiful desert on earth. Eilat's a pretty stinking city; it is really hot and the air is dry. But the beaches are beautiful and there are dolphins and everything. That's not even the point: The mountains of Eilat are the most amazing place in this world. It's so peaceful and quiet there. No plants, no nothing. You could just sit there and it would be very, very quiet and you would hear nothing. It is amazing. I traveled a lot in Israel, with my movement and with my family. My family went camping for our summer vacation, or I went on trips with *Shomer HaZair* all over the country. I have done some traveling in America and Europe. There are beautiful places there. It's always green in Europe. But here we have the deserts, places where it's really quiet and nobody is there for kilometers around. There is nothing to worry about; no buses ever blew up in the desert.

If you like the Mediterranean, well, we have that, too. I love deserts, also the Judean Desert close to Jerusalem. I love it when you can just be somewhere and be quiet and hear nothing. Nothing at all. No crickets, no birds. Think of a place that seems like no one ever set foot there and where you won't find a big "M" somewhere for McDonalds. So if anyone comes to Israel I really recommend the mountains of Eilat. It is nice to live in a country that has a lot of desert with all those different plants and things. There are distinct advantages to being "waterless."

I love those trips my movement is organizing. To the north, to camp on a small river. Yes, we have a river, the Banyas on the Golan Heights. We would make a small grill in the ground, and bake the food in there, which is really fun. I like traveling and environmental challenges. I am a really lazy person, but when it comes to traveling I am out there.

After the army, I really want to travel to South America because my father is from Argentina and I want to go there so-o-o much. Also I saw a TV show about Peru and I just thought: I want to go there, too. The landscape was breathtaking and the people seemed to be so friendly. I also know a little Spanish and I want to learn Spanish fluently. I would love to walk among the natives and speak Spanish with them. Also, because I don't have much money and still want to spend much time abroad, South America would really be great.

China is another place I would like to go to. I would like to know where you would love to go. I am aware that there are some problems when Palestinians want to move around. I can imagine that it is not that easy, especially now that the Americans are in that war against terror after September 11. Arabs and Muslims in general have to suffer so many more restrictions and biases.

I know that you might have problems with traveling. If I didn't have the opportunity to travel in my country or around the world, I would probably feel like an animal in a cage. I just hope for a better future. I try to pass on the values I believe in to the kids I am working with and hope that they will make the world better for everyone. And I hope that you will have more opportunities to travel and feel free to do your own thing. Perhaps you would like to travel in the desert to get away from everything, even if it were only for an hour.

Yours,
Odelia

مجزرة شارون: ١٢ شهيداً، بينهم أطفال ونساء، و١٥٠ جريحاً في غزة

Al Hayat, July 24, 2002
Sharon's Massacre: 12 Martyrs, Among Them Babies and Women Killed in
Gaza; 150 Wounded

*Amal*
*September 8, 2002.*

Dear Odelia,
Like you, I love traveling; I love to get to know different
places. But I am uncomfortable traveling, even in my own
country, because most of the areas I would like to go to are
closed off to me. What a disturbing feeling that I cannot
even get to know the towns and villages in my own country.

My older brother studies at Bir Zeit University, which is
close to Ramallah. It's a major trip every time he comes
home or he wants to go back to the university. Sometimes
he has to wait for hours at an Israeli checkpoint. Sometimes,
when he finally reaches the checkpoint, the soldiers ask him
all sorts of questions or turn him back. Sometimes a soldier
does him a favor and lets him pass. But then he might get
stuck in Ramallah because he's barred from going back. He
has to use all sorts of dirt roads or walk through the fields
just to get back home.

Do they restrict people on purpose, consigning them to a
life of frustration and boredom at home? To me it seems
that they like to play with people's nerves until they finally

explode. I don't see any other way than to fight all this. I am getting furious just thinking about being treated badly at a checkpoint.

So, you want to get away from all this. As if it were that easy. My family and I have Jordanian passports, which means that for every trip, even to Jordan, we need to have a *laissez-passer,* a travel document issued by the Israeli Ministry of Interior. My brother and I wanted to go to America this summer. So he went to the Ministry the evening before to reserve a place in line for the next morning. The Ministry opens its doors at eight in the morning; in the afternoon he finally reached the counter. The whole morning he had to wait in the baking sun; there is nothing there to protect people from the heat in the summer or the cold and rain in the winter. Sometimes they just close the counter right before it's your turn because the office hours are over for the day. Or people apply and are declined a travel document for some unexplained "security reasons." Nobody ever has the chance to find out on what grounds they were refused a travel document or what exactly the "security reasons" are. This is suffering that no one can take. Even when you only ask for a form for a *laissez-passer,* you have to wait hours.

This is how I am trapped in my own country. I cannot move around inside because of army checkpoints and I cannot move outside because of Israeli bureaucracy. I have the feeling that they want to give me a hard time on purpose before I leave the country and have some fun. This is what makes me sometimes despair of even thinking of traveling. Instead of going abroad and having to suffer all those bureaucratic tortures, I would rather stay home and be bored.

13 אזרחים, בהם 9 ילדים, נהרגו בהתנקשות בבכיר החמאס שחאדה

בצה"ל יבדקו את הסיבות לכישלון הפעולה בעזה

Haaretz, July 24, 2002
Thirteen Civilians, Among Them Nine Children Killed During Raid at Hamas-Leader Shahada
**Subhead:** Army Orders Investigation on Reasons for Failure of Operation in Gaza

This summer, however, I finally went to a place that is far away from bloodshed and barbaric treatment. Since I could not get a visa to the United States, my family and I decided to spend out summer vacation in Jordan where we have lots of relatives. It's one of the few places in the world where we don't need a visa. We got up just before sunrise to get to the Allenby Bridge early. We arrived at seven and waited for an hour until the border crossing was opened. Three hours later we finally had crossed the few meters over the bridge. Israeli border police check everybody's luggage really thoroughly.

Do you know what a relief that was to just go out without fearing I would be stopped by somebody and asked all sorts of questions—what are you doing here, where do you come from, what's your name, show me your ID? I am wondering what they need police for in Jordan, because nobody is ever checked there in the streets. I don't doubt that my homeland is more beautiful than Jordan. It's the place I grew up in, the place that is familiar to me and close to my heart. But all of us enjoyed the peaceful atmosphere in Jordan. My whole family felt so relaxed, as if we finally had left a prison. I felt like a bird freed from its cage, as free as a human being is supposed to be.

On one of the first days of my stay in Jordan, my aunt and I went to the market. Forgetting where I was for the moment, I asked her whether she had her ID with her. She looked at me as if I were out of my mind and then laughed. "Here in Jordan we don't have to carry our ID with us all the time. I don't even know where I placed mine." That stunned me. And I envied her. I thought about whether I could act like her in Israel. What would I say if a policeman asked me for my ID? Would he believe me when I said I had just left it at home? Not very likely. Just thinking that I could lose my blue ID, which entitles me to live in my birthplace, Jerusalem, gives me the shivers.

Jordan is a great and beautiful country. You can do everything you want to without being stopped or having people constantly looking suspiciously at your bag or wanting to search it. The most precious feeling to me was that in Jordan I could understand everybody in the streets, and I could be understood by everybody, since we all speak the same language. Not like home, where people look at you suspiciously and with animosity or even hatred when you speak Arabic. I loved going out and having fun without being stopped even one time. I could move around there as I pleased. But it is not the place where I was born, and where I grew up. With all this cultural familiarity, with all the relatives of mine whom I dearly love around me, it's still not my home, and I am just considered a stranger. Just like at home where I am

considered a stranger in my own land. I seem to have the word *stranger* written all over my forehead.
Amal


*Odelia*
*September 16, 2002*


Dear Amal,
Everything you wrote—I know. I know what's going on in this country. I know how bad Arabs are treated in Israel. When "the situation" started, I talked to friends and we said, "Oh, I wouldn't want to be an Arab in this country now. They probably get a lot of trouble." Now I know about it and it makes me very angry and upset. I have many discussions about it with my friends and family. I am totally aware of the problems. But, again, it's such a difficult situation.

A soldier is an eighteen-, nineteen-, or twenty-year-old who has to face terrible issues on his own. You never know if a man standing at a barrier is a suicide bomber or not. I wouldn't want to face that problem. I wouldn't want to tell an ambulance to turn back because it might have a bomb or something. It is difficult. These "soldiers" are kids who just finished school and now might become responsible for the death of some civilians, just because they followed some orders.

I think the problem lies in the somewhat arrogant attitude of many Israeli Jews, who feel that it is not essential to find a compromise with the Arabs, and that the Palestinians should not get what they deserve, and what we took from them. Moreover, some think that because of the war we have now, the Arabs should be treated even worse because they are "potential suicide bombers." Of course this is a generalization. Not all Israeli Jews think like that. I think the idea of an Arab in Israeli society should change. Arabs were never considered equals in our society. There is a saying: "You can always find a poorer man than you." Even if you were the poorest person in the world, you would find someone on whom you could take out your aggressions or someone to "come down on." That's the way our society is built. Lessons from the past were not learned, and racism and discrimination still exist and are very much alive all over the world.

I don't have a solution. People must understand for themselves that they must change their way of thinking. But it seems to me that they want to stick with this situation by becoming more and more radical and extreme in their ideas.

Yours,

Odelia

# Five

## DISCUSSION BETWEEN AMAL AND ODELIA

After more than a month of communicating only by writing, Amal and Odelia wanted to meet and talk to each other directly because some topics require quicker answers. Both also felt the urge to express their respect and affection for each other, which they had developed in their first round of letter writing. As the moderator for this conversation, I wanted to use this opportunity to tackle some issues that—in my opinion at least—had not yet been addressed.

*Jerusalem, October, 1, 2002*

**AMAL:** You know, when we were in Switzerland, my friend Samira kept telling me all the time that you were very nice. But I didn't like the whole group. After we made contact again and after I read your first letters, I thought I was wrong. You are so-o different than who I thought you were. If there were more people like you, I guess we really could live together.

**ODELIA:** Thank you. Also, many things became clearer to me when you started to talk about your personal life and things weren't that abstract anymore.

**AMAL:** I basically grew up with the idea that the Israelis are out there to kill us. I was surprised to find out that you know a few things about our life and that you try to understand how the situation is for us. I liked the sound of your family; they are obviously different. Sorry, but it still seems to me as if they aren't Israelis at all.

**ODELIA:** There are lots of people like them. Well, perhaps not lots, but, at least, let's say 20 percent of society.

**AMAL:** You know I will start to love the Israelis.

**ODELIA (laughs):** Oh no! What have I done?

**AMAL:** OK, I am joking. But I do like my Jewish friends from *Peace Child Israel;* I went with the group to visit Akko. It does make a difference to meet some people, because usually I don't speak to Israelis. Or my encounters are rather unpleasant. The other day, I had to introduce myself to the headmaster of the college I want to go to. I knock, enter the room, nicely say Hello, and this Mrs. Levi or whatever her name is tells me: "Don't you see that I am busy right now? Can't you come back some other time?" I told her: "What? I made this trip from the other side of the city and you tell me to come back some other time?" I flipped, turned around and told her, "Thank you, I won't come back again." See, you can't talk to those Israelis.

**ODELIA:** But those people would do that to everyone. Israelis are not known for being too polite. They would be impolite to me, too.

**AMAL:** Perhaps I take things too personally. Especially when I was a bit younger, I was sure that it was because the other person was Israeli and I was an Arab. I am beginning to understand, though, that rudeness is not always meant personally.

**ODELIA:** The other day I had a political discussion with my mother. I told her that I thought it was wrong that we don't learn something about Arab culture. But then she told me that, in general, we always had seen the Arabs as the enemy. Why would we learn the language of the enemy? Why would we study their culture? She knows and understands some Arabic because of her Moroccan background. I guess she makes a point. Only in the last couple of years did we study Arabic in school. And only then did we begin to understand that the Arabs are not just our enemies but the ones we have to live with—and are living with.

**AMAL:** When I gave my daddy your letters to read, he said: "You know, I was always for living with the Israelis because there is no other option anyway. And if they would give us what belongs to us, I am sure each side would leave the other alone and probably there would be no bombs." For me it is always about equality.

**SYLKE TEMPEL:** When you talk about equality, Amal, does it mean you would like to be an equal Israeli citizen or would you like to be a Palestinian citizen in a Palestinian state?

**ODELIA:** Lots of Arabs who are Israeli citizens, or even many who live in Jerusalem like you without having Israeli citizen-

ship, consider themselves Palestinians and still would not like
to live in a Palestinian state.

**AMAL:** Of course, because the situation there is very bad.

**ODELIA:** And because their government is pretty bad and cor-
rupt.

**AMAL:** What's most important to me is this: I want to live a
life in peace and quiet. Living in Jerusalem means that I am
under Israeli rule and that, if I don't want real trouble I must
obey their laws. And, that I will have to pay my taxes to the
Israeli authorities as my father does.

**ODELIA:** But I think that the Palestinians should have their
state! I also think that the Palestinian Authority wasn't very
good at building that state . . .

**AMAL:** But look at places like Ramallah. What a nice city it
was, but the Israelis have destroyed it! Why would you build
and invest in the future if everything was going to be destroyed anyway!? Why not, then, invest in weapons and en-
gage in armed struggle?

**ODELIA:** I also mean building the institutions for a state. Yes,
we are there and are destroying a lot. But the Palestinians
weren't very successful in building the institutions for a state
before the Intifada either. If we leave the Territories and
there is a Palestinian state one day, it is going to be a pretty
poor one under this leadership.

**AMAL:** Yes, the Palestinian government is pretty poor, and sometimes I think it would have to go before there could be peace. We gave up what belonged to us, and people just want what the Israelis took in 1967. But I don't think too highly of the Palestinian government. Yassir Arafat is our president and nobody knows where he comes from. We don't know his family, we don't clearly know his origins.

**ST:** You were both born in Jerusalem, you both love the city, and both Palestinians and Israelis want to have it as their capital. How would you resolve that?

**AMAL:** I just want to go to the Friday prayers on Haram al Sharif without being checked by soldiers. My father went to the prayers the other Friday. Six prayers are obligatory, but he could only do four because he heard gunshots and started to worry about my mother, who was in the women's section. He really panicked! He looked for her and, after he finally found her, they went home as quickly as possible.

**ODELIA:** If there were a peace agreement and I wanted to visit Palestine, well, then, I would cross a real border and show my passport. I wouldn't mind crossing a border before I could go to the Wailing Wall.

**AMAL:** *Achlan we Sachlan* [welcome to our house]. You can come to Palestine any time.

**ODELIA:** It could be like crossing into Sinai: Here is my passport, you get it stamped, have a nice day, that's it. We would have a real border with some border crossing. In Europe there are borders you almost don't notice.

**AMAL:** Wasn't that great, when we traveled from Switzerland to Italy? We weren't even checked. And here it took me fifteen days just to get my visa, and that's considered a short time.

**ST:** It took Europe fifty years after a horrible war to unify and to create open borders. Besides, there are no, let's say, Italian suicide bombers infiltrating Austria.

**ODELIA:** I know that I'm talking about utopia.

**AMAL:** The Israeli governments always talked about peace, and they might have signed some papers, but there was no real peace. Sometimes I think to myself that we never will live together in peace and quiet—basically every time something happens in Ramallah or in Bethlehem or in Gaza. I come home again only to ask my daddy about how many Palestinians got killed again, and I sit glued to the TV. To me it is normal to see people killed, something as ordinary as eating chocolate. Then I am absolutely convinced there never will be real peace. But when I am sitting with people like you, or my friends from *Peace Child Israel*, I have hope again that we could somehow manage it. We are a group of a few dozen. I have my doubts though that the almost 10 million Palestinians and Israelis here could manage it.

**ODELIA:** The problem is the people from both sides who want to fight in order to win. There is no concept of enjoying life. It has to be about "winning" and an attitude like that is encouraged by both governments. And what is this stupid notion of "winning" anyway? That the other side is just "Gone with the Wind," vanished, disappeared?

**ST:** Do you remember that, before the Intifada, there was a time people did not talk about "fighting" or "winning," but really had hopes for peace?

**ODELIA:** I think we were too young.

**AMAL:** I remember the days after the first Intifada and before this one. I watched the first one on TV and did not yet really understand what was going on. It was over when I was only eight or nine years old and not much older when the Oslo agreement was signed. I didn't follow the news that closely after the first Intifada. Daddy told me that the situation got better and that we could live together. We went to Ramallah, which was possible because there were almost no checkpoints at the time. I also saw the Palestinian policemen, but I couldn't really figure out what they were there for. I was far too young; I didn't understand. Besides, Daddy wants us to have a happy and quiet life. This is why he doesn't want us to deal with politics too much. He doesn't want us to end up as fighters.

**ODELIA:** I remember my parents went everywhere, and definitely there weren't people around to constantly check your bags . . .

**AMAL:** . . . And we would do all our shopping in Ramallah, we could go there three times a day. But still there were checkpoints. My daddy and I went to Ramallah one day, and we saw an Arab woman in traditional dress. A soldier asked her to open her coat so he would be sure she wasn't carrying anything. She refused, so he hit her with his gun. She spat at him. My father didn't want me to look. But in 1994 and 1995 it was so much easier to go to Jordan. It was shortly after the peace agreement and it was so easy to get through. They just screened our bags—that's it. Now it's such a hassle.

**ST:** If it was so much better then, how do you explain the reasons for the situation now?

**ODELIA:** Probably because we both can't overcome this stupid idea of settling our disputes by violence. And then, of course, the discrimination and frustration were not over; I don't think our attitudes have changed much. I guess it is just so easy to push those buttons because we have been fighting this war for such a long time. Only now, people are beginning to understand again that there are other options. That we could get out of this idiotic cycle of "You hit me so I hit you back." There are lots of people by now who do not want to go to the army or at least want to change something for the better from within. Slowly we are changing our attitude from one of arrogance: "We came here, this is our land, and we are so much better because their culture is so strange," and we are slowly coming to understand their culture and how to deal with people who are different.

**AMAL:** Sometimes I also ask myself if somebody has prepared us for other options than just violence. My history teacher explained the history of the conflict like this: This is our land; the Jews came here and stole it from us. One of the reason for their success was, so he said: While the Arab women were at home preparing dinner for the family, the Jewish women learned to use guns. And only if we also learn to use guns can we get it back. I once had an argument with an Israeli boy in *Peace Child Israel,* who told me, "This is our land and the Wailing Wall was there and ours for thousands of years." But I told him that he still did not have a right to steal our land. He just walked away.

**ODELIA:** That's the problem with ignorant people who just make statements and then walk away. You cannot discuss matters with them seriously. The thing is, right now it is our land, too. My mom also said she wouldn't have cared if our state had been built in Uganda [see Chronology]. But now it's here. She was born here, and so were my sisters, my brother, and I.

# Six

## JERUSALEM

*Odelia*
*September 30, 2002*

Dear Amal,
I really really love Jerusalem. With the situation, it is more complicated now, with all the bombings. But overall it is a pretty easygoing town. Before the war lots of tourists came— not only for religious reasons, but also just for the "tourist stuff": Jerusalem is not exactly like London or Paris.

It is also not like Tel Aviv, always noisy and "hip." It is more relaxed. Sometimes I feel as if I were in a kibbutz: I walk through the same places and I meet the same people over and over. Before I moved to Kfar Saba, I always took the same bus in Jerusalem and always the same route. You always have the same people on the bus saying Hello, talking about what's happening; you feel as if you know everybody. I always liked having a regular way of doing things, a regular day—you get up the same hour every day, you take the same bus at the same hour, go to the same movie theater in the evening, and meet the same people. You can move around and don't have to put on airs. In Tel Aviv, I always feel as if people around me are trying to show some attitude. "We are so cool; we live in Tel Aviv," and we are going to the beach and we are all tan and have the best cars. People don't do that in Jerusalem. I know there are many people who think it is a boring city. I don't think it is boring at all and right now, if you think of the situation, it is probably the least boring city in the world.

Many people wonder: What's there to do in Jerusalem? But I love those quiet little pubs where we have music and you talk to people and you could go to bars that are a little bigger, but everywhere you have the feeling that you are so familiar with the places and the people, you feel so connected. You walk down those little streets and it feels so peaceful despite the problems. Especially on Yom Kippur, I like to walk around the city that for one day in the year is totally "car free." Jerusalem has these different alleyways that wind up and down the hills, small streets with old houses, so many different parts. It is, you could say, one city divided between many different people. From where I grew up, I could walk to an Arab neighborhood in five minutes. I would only be walking that short a distance, but I would be walking from what I know, from my world, to a completely different environment.

Also, the Old City of Jerusalem is amazing. I haven't been there for two years. The first time I went there again was when we took the photos for this book. Oh my God—I felt that I was out of the country in some faraway land. I walked past the walls and I thought to myself: That's part of the town I live in? And I haven't been here for two years because of the situation and because my parents will not let me. The only reason I could go there now is because my parents and I have the feeling: If we go with the press, nobody will do anything to me." But you have everything there and everything is so unique. And then I think to myself: How could anyone think that Jerusalem is boring? You could always find a new place you haven't been to before and always find some crazy, weird alley. You could walk up an alley and at the end you could find some very old house with some explanation saying that this house was built two hundred years ago and you wouldn't even know. And there are some bad things—like the city hall, which really looks awful, and the streets are filthy, and all that political and bureaucratic business. Some of the old houses are neglected and the city is not as well taken care of as it should be. But, all in all, I feel really connected to Jerusalem.

To think that not all, but a lot of what is going on is because of Jerusalem is really strange. I understand why people want Jerusalem. But, then, I am not connected to Jerusalem because of the history. I am connected to it because I was born there and I lived there for most of my life. I don't live there now, and I miss it so much. Not only do I miss my home, but I miss the feeling of the city. It is such a big city, burdened with so many conflicts, but inside you can find so many interesting, quiet places. I really love that city. Both my parents lived in Tel Aviv for some time. They met there. My mom comes from Jerusalem, and when they decided to get married, she said to my father: If we want to have kids, then we will move to Jerusalem because I am not going to raise my kids in any other city. And I understand that. I know that Europeans or Americans probably would not understand it, because they think it is so dangerous. Come on—New York is also dangerous, perhaps even more so. If you are

كتائب القسام تتبناها:

## مقتل سبعة أشخاص وإصابة ٨٦ آخرين
## في انفجار عبوة داخل مطعم في الجامعة العبرية

Al Hayat, August 1, 2002
Al Kassam Brigades Declare Responsibility:
Seven Killed and 86 Wounded by Explosion of Bomb in Hebrew University
Cafeteria

born in Jerusalem, you are connected to it. And the Jerusalemites know what I am talking about. It is this love for a city
that has everything in it. If you are looking for a crowd of
cool, "happening" people who go to hip places, you can find
that. If you want a crowd of Muslims, there you go; Christians, there they are. Whatever you want, you've got it. And
some religious fanatics, too.

It is really difficult sometimes to explain to people who do
not come from Jerusalem why I love the city, even though
it is in this current, extremely problematic situation. I mean,
with all the bombings. You don't know how many times I,
or my friends, or someone from my family was close to getting hurt. I know people who did get hurt, or were at a place
where a bombing took place only a few minutes before, or
were right there and then decided to quickly go get something and that was how they got away. It's frightening, of
course, because I don't feel free. It doesn't mean I am afraid
all the time; I do walk down the streets and enjoy the beauty
of the city. But the cafés—it is so sad now; cafés were closed
because of the situation. There were some neat ones located
in some old houses built from Jerusalem stone, so cozy that

7 הרוגים בפיצוץ מטען באוניברסיטה
העברית; 2 קרובי מחבלים יגורשו לעזה

Haaretz, August 1, 2002
Seven Killed by Bomb Attacks at Hebrew University Cafeteria; Two Members
of Palestinian Terror Group to be Exiled to Gaza

you had the feeling you could go there in your pajamas and
slippers and read a book or play cards and have the best
feeling in your life by just enjoying yourself without having
to put on airs or anything.

I heard fanatics on television, I mean from Hamas, and
they were saying stuff like: "We can't have Jews here, we
have to kick them out, and they have to go back where they
came from." Hello? I came from Jerusalem. That's my home.
Period. And I know that I want to go everywhere and live
in all sorts of different places in the world. But I will always
remember Jerusalem and I will always go back to it. Not
because of all this religious stuff and the spiritual, historical
meaning, but because *it is my home.* I was born there, I
know it, my friends are from there and my language, my
accent or dialect, is spoken there. I don't know if you know
this, but Jerusalemites have their own dialect or slang. It is
really funny. But when we had trips with my youth organization, the other kids would notice: Oh, look at the Jerusalemites, they speak another dialect, how funny—and always
laughed at us. People from Jerusalem always consider themselves different because there's always a reaction to them

when the say they are from Jerusalem. So, nobody can tell me: Go back where you came from, because this is the place I come from, and this is the place I was born. And maybe the way we built this country and the way we occupied the country is not right and not moral, but it happened and I don't have anywhere else to go. My language is Hebrew and Israel is the only place where they speak Hebrew. My money is shekels; I convert an amount into shekels when I have to buy something in dollars, pounds, or whatever currency. My feelings, my jokes, my attitude are Israeli and Jerusalemite. Here is my home.

I know that my father wasn't born here and my mother's mother wasn't born here. But it is their home, too, now. My father never went back to Argentina after he left it, and he does not intend to go back. For twenty-something years, Israel has been his home. His children speak Hebrew, not Spanish. His children count money in shekels, sing Israeli songs, and watch Israeli television. They live in Jerusalem and know how to take a bus from one place to another. They know where to walk or where to find the best cafés. Their friends speak Jerusalem slang, they go to the cinemathèque. This is where kids meet because it's cool there. I love the place; at the same time, I hate what's going on. I hate that I see discrimination in the streets and on the buses and I hear all those stupid, racist, annoying jokes. But I hate it also when some fanatic comes and says: "Go back where you came from" when there is no "back." There is no way; there is no place where I can go "back." And all I want is just to be able to live in Jerusalem in true peace. It's not about stupid treaties but about an understanding that you and I, Amal, we both want to live here.

You, Amal, don't have anywhere else to go. But neither do I. And everywhere else I go, I also feel uneasy and like a stranger. I truly want to live with the Arabs and I want them to have a state. The fact that perhaps half of this country or more doesn't want this is a problem, and they really have to change their attitude. I am here and I want to see a change in attitude, but I also want the other side to understand that I do know my city and I love it because I was born here. It's a home I really truly want to share because I understand that it is also home to a lot of other people. I know it. But we can't turn history back now, and there is no place else in the world I feel a hundred percent comfortable; the only place where I feel a hundred percent at home is Jerusalem. I know how to talk, to act, to find my way.

I hope you will understand that this is why I am saying: We both want to live here because it is home for you and for me. Because I understand that this is the place where your ancestors lived. But it is a place that also means a lot to us and is part of our ancient history. Certainly many things went wrong between Arabs and Israelis in the last fifty years. But I wasn't here fifty years ago; I was born eighteen years ago. That's why we have to learn to live together. Even if it sounds like a bumper sticker.

Yours,

Odelia

*Amal*
*October 4, 2002*

Dear Odelia,

I also like the Old City very much. I love to walk on the city walls. I love to go to the Friday prayers on the Haram al Sharif. This is something that really excites me. Especially during Ramadan, we love to go there after the fast break. It is so beautiful with the stars above us, the most beautiful to me is the Night of Destiny (the night from the 26th to the 27th day of Ramadan). Every Muslim in the country tries to come to pray on the Haram al-Sharif this very special night, because it's holy to us Muslims. It is impressive to see all these people coming from all different parts of the country. This night, praying under the star-lit sky of *Al-Kuds* [Arab name for Jerusalem], you feel that you are truly close to God.

Yes, living in Jerusalem teaches you a bit about people of other faiths, just from the daily experience. When I was little, I would wonder why shops were closed on Saturdays. Then Daddy told me that it was a holiday for religious Jews. They close everything and stay at home, he told me. In some neighborhoods, they even shut down the roads. But we Muslims are not affected by it. We could go anywhere except into those religious neighborhoods. I basically learned from my daddy about the Jewish holidays. He was working with Jewish Israelis and sometimes he stayed at home. Than he explained to me that there were more holidays, like Sukkot, Purim, and Pesach.

In school we also learned something about Jewish history. After all, I took the Israeli Bagrut exam. I remember that there were Jewish minorities in almost every country in the world and that everywhere they encountered animosity. They suffered persecution perhaps because nobody really wanted them. We also learned something about the beginning of Zionism and Theodor Herzl's vision of a Jewish state. And that there were plans to build that state in Argentina or even Uganda. I have difficulty understanding the religious connection of the Jews with this land. I mean, we learned at school that the first Zionists who came here did not care at all about their religion but just wanted to build their country. So, naturally, I wonder why they then would come here and not go to Uganda or Argentina. We Arabs believe that they came here because the land was rich. *Falastin* means "rich country." All this talk about the religious connection, all these things about the Temple in Jerusalem and the Wailing Wall there seem a bit artificial to me.

After the Israelis had conquered the West Bank, all of a sudden they were digging all over the place and finding all these remnants from their religion. We studied some of the Bible in class, but actually we were not really interested in that. It was hard for me because I am a Muslim and not Jewish. I just memorized it because we needed to know it for the Bagrut exam. Perhaps there might be a historical connection, but wasn't there a Jewish history in many other countries? See, our experience is that after the War of 1948, many Arab towns were conquered and things all of a sudden changed. Now there was no Arab connection anymore but only a Jewish one. Besides, in our classes we learned more about Palestine and its Muslim history and not about Jewish history.

It is very interesting: I meet Israeli kids and some of them tell me that their parents or grandparents come from France or Russia. Some Israelis even come from Ethiopia. But when you ask them, "Where are you from?" they always say, "From Israel." If you asked a Palestinian kid where he came from, he'd say, "From Palestine" no matter where he lived, inside or outside Palestine. Or he'd say he was from the town or village that his parents and grandparents came from, even if they were living in a refugee camp. If you asked somebody Jewish, they would always say they come from Israel, even though their parents were from Russia or someplace else. To my way of thinking, you come from where your father and grandfather were born. Somebody whose grandparents, for example, moved from Hebron to Jerusalem would still be considered a Hebronite. Our feeling is: You take somebody's home, the place he and all his ancestors were born, and you take his life.

Come to think of it: I really never had the feeling that I wanted to delve so deeply into Jewish or Israeli history in order to understand what makes Jews tick. I feel that I know it from my daily encounters and from what I see in the news.

Besides, I feel that I know more about the Israelis than the Israelis know about me. They are the rulers, I have to abide by their rules and as you, Odelia, had said, you Israelis don't learn a lot about our customs, traditions, or history at school.

I know some of the Jewish holidays, while most Israelis don't have a clue about our feasts and holidays. Besides, the ancient Jewish history doesn't mean a thing to me. What matters to me is what happened in the last hundred years with the beginning of the Zionist movement. And since the

Zionists came here, I would think it would be their obligation
to study our customs and not the other way around.
I hope you understand.
Amal

*Odelia*
*October 22, 2002*

Dear Amal,
It is a pity that you did not really want to delve more deeply
into the history of the Jews in this country. I very often said
that I regret not having learned more about the Muslim-Arab
history here. I think it is necessary for each of us to learn
something about the other.

To me, the Bible is really a sort of thrilling "history book."
I read it with a critical approach and I certainly don't believe
everything written in there. I love most the book *Cohelet*
[Book of Solomon]. It is like a piece of literature to me,
something I like to read and think about thoroughly. Reading
the Bible makes you feel connected with this land; Jerusalem
is mentioned so many times in there. And it is not, as you
write, that "after 1967 the Jews all of a sudden found all
those remnants of their history in the West Bank." Many, if
not most, of the events in the Bible are historical. There are
many archaeological studies about that, not only conducted
by Israeli scientists.

I am certainly not very religious, but the connection between us and the land also means something to me. I love
Jerusalem much better than Kfar Saba, which was only built
in modern Israel. Jerusalem is so old and so important to

many religions, and because so many different people live here. I love Jerusalem because it has meaning in our history.

I very much hope Jerusalem remains a cosmopolitan city and a home for many different religions and ethnic groups.

I think it is amazing that so many people of different national backgrounds could come here and create something like an Israeli culture. My father might be from Argentina and my mother's parents from Morocco. But certainly neither my sisters and brother nor I are Argentinian or Moroccan. We are Israelis through and through. When the Swiss were here, they were absolutely astonished that we have Israeli songs. Songs, written and sung in Hebrew that are incredibly popular here. They said in Switzerland there weren't any Swiss-German songs, only English ones. There is so much Israeli culture here—books, films, TV shows that are typically Israeli. I love all this. It also deeply connects me with this land.

It concerns me that so many people seem to misunderstand our religion. I don't understand, for example, why the settlers of Hebron insist on living there, only because Hebron was part of Jewish history. It's irrational and not very moral. Every day they are endangering their own and other people's lives because there are clashes. To me it is incomprehensible that our army has to protect these settlements in Hebron. Or that they would carry huge blocks of concrete in there, as I have recently seen on TV, to build an enormous wall between themselves and the hundred thousand Palestinians living there. I don't think that all of this could be justified by the texts of the Bible. In Judaism, saving a life is much more important than anything else. This is why I believe that many of the really beautiful principles of our religion are misunderstood. I find it utterly incomprehensible that a piece of land or a settlement in Hebron could be more important than a human life. I think that's totally wrong.

I think there are many beautiful ideas in Judaism. And certainly there is a connection between the Jews and this land.

My mother might have said that it would not have made a difference to her whether the Jewish state was built here or in Uganda. It was meant as a joke. For both of my parents, Israel was very important, for different reasons. They met in Tel Aviv, fell in love, got married, had four children—three girls and a boy; I am the oldest. To think that without Israel they would not have met. Here is their story.

Yours,

Odelia

*Enri and Mazal Ainbinder Tell Their Stories*

**ENRI:** I was born in Cordoba, one of the big cities in Argentina with more than 1 million inhabitants. As in Jerusalem, life in Cordoba was quiet and slow without the hectic rush of a "city that never sleeps" like Buenos Aires or Tel Aviv.

Argentina's first university was founded in my hometown. Therefore, it was called *Cordoba la Docta*—Cordoba the Learned. It was also home to one of the largest Jewish communities in Argentina. We had a Jewish primary and secondary school and, like most of the Jewish kids in Cordoba, I went to the Jewish school.

Students learned according to the Argentine curriculum, but in addition to that, the history of Israel was taught as well as Bible and Jewish History—and all of it in Hebrew!

In fact, this school was like two in one, including faculty and principal. One for the Hebrew curriculum, one for the Argentine. We also celebrated all Jewish, Israeli, and Argentine festivities. Which meant that we would raise both the Argentine and the Israeli flags and sing both national anthems.

In the mid-1960s, a Zionist-socialist youth movement was established in the city. I joined the movement when I was twelve or thirteen.

We organized a lot of activities together: Saturday's meetings, picnics, summer camps, and winter seminars. We had many discussions about socialism, and Zionism, and we wanted to make *aliyah* [immigrate to Israel] as a *garin* ["nucleus," a group of people the same age] and join a kibbutz.

We were Zionist-socialist; it was not out of the religious connection that we wanted to immigrate to Israel but because of our ideology.

We really believed that in order to become a "normal" people we had to turn the society upside down: We Jews shouldn't be so concentrated in the bourgeois professions; we should also become workers, and the place where we wanted to create the "new man" and a truly socialist society was Israel. It was quite clear that at the ages of eighteen through twenty we would go to Israel as a group of young new pioneers. At that time we were great idealists.

I even decided to study agronomy because my idea was go to the kibbutz and to work the land.

At this time, everyone in the whole world knew about the kibbutz—this socialist and very successful experiment of people who live and work together; where children are raised by the whole community; where everybody cooperates in the building of a new society; and where truly democratic decisions are made by all members of the kibbutz.

But all these dreams of immigrating to Israel as a group came to a dramatic end when the Argentine army staged a coup d'état and replaced the democratically elected government with a military regime in 1976. The last group of *garin,* or pioneers for Israel, had left a year before. After the coup d'état, all the political and even social groups and youth movements were declared illegal. Few of the members of my group left in the winter of '76, and the movement ceased to exist. This was the time of the *desaparecidos.* People were arrested by the security forces, and simply "disappeared," never to be heard from again.

At the end of 1977, I immigrated to Israel, alone, as a student. My first two months I spent on a kibbutz. But the kibbutz wasn't the place I had dreamt it would be. There were fights within the community, intrigues, and they had paid workers! The people we envisioned as the nucleus of socialism, the examples for the new world, were really managers, and they had hired paid workers!

After two months, I left for Jerusalem to study at the university. I lived in a dormitory on Shmuel Hanavi Street. Jerusalem was such a crazy, wonderful place—full of young students from all over the world, from both North and South America, Europe, Australia, even Iran. All of us tried very hard to speak this impossible Hebrew language. Each and every one of us was happy when we managed to ask for an address and the bus driver understood us. And we were even happier when we could understand what he'd said to us! There were few places in these days to go out to in Jerusalem: Pizza Rimini, the cinematheque, and the Old City. We would walk from our hostel to the Swedish Tea House, close to Jaffa Gate, or to Abu Shukri for the best hummus in the city. Very often we would walk back home in the middle of the night and none of us ever felt uncomfortable or were afraid. It was absolutely natural for us to go to the Old City, stroll around in those narrow alleys, shop in the bazaar, or have something to eat in those little restaurants.

In Cordoba, we had heard stories from the Israelis who came to Argentina to encourage *aliyah* [immigration to Israel]. They kept on saying: "Israel is a Jewish country. It is wonderful, beautiful, we have everything you want, and we have built it in only thirty years!" *Wow!*

When I came here I had to face the real Israel. Well, it is certainly not paradise, but also not worse than other places in the world. We might not have "everything you want" here, but you can find almost everything you need. And that's not a small thing.

Why did I come here? I was an idealist; I strongly believed in the ideal of building a socialist society in Israel, and also all my friends had left Argentina. When I look at Israel today, I would say: No, we did not succeed in building a socialist society; Israel is far from this ideal. But I have built my life here: I never thought about going back to Argentina. I left the place and everything there behind me.

My sister came to Israel a year before me, then she got married. Then I married Mazal, and when my parents realized we were not coming back, they followed us.

They immigrated in 1983, and had to build a new life for themselves, learn the language, and even get new jobs. They were already in their mid-fifties and it was anything but easy for them. But it happens very often here that the parents come after their kids.

**MAZAL:** When I met Enri I thought: It is so strange that he is Jewish, yet he does not know a thing about the Jewish religion. I came from a traditional family.

My grandfather Eliyahu was a rabbi in Morocco. He owned a small factory for handmade soap. I never met him. He died before I was born, but I heard all these stories about him.

He desperately wanted to be here. One of his daughters, my aunt Sultana, or Malka, as she was called in Israel, had already immigrated to Jerusalem in 1937 and they constantly exchanged letters. My mother told me that he always said, "If I should die in Morocco, I at least want to be buried in Jerusalem." When, after the creation of Israel, the harassment of the Jews in Morocco became worse, my grandfather finally decided to come here.

He was already over eighty years old when he came here in 1951 with his family. My mother was just seventeen years old; she was my grandfather's daughter from his second marriage.

Many Jews from Morocco had to travel through France, where my grandfather spent a whole month in a transit camp until he could board a ship to Israel. When he finally arrived here, he knelt down and kissed the soil of the Holy Land of which he had always dreamed. My father, may he rest in peace, finally came to Israel in 1949, after he had tried to make it to Israel on his own many times before. Once he crossed the border into Algeria illegally and was sent back. Another time he dressed up in traditional Arab clothes so as not to be recognized as a Jew. But all these attempts to come to Israel on his own failed. Finally, he arrived with his family via France. They had to wait in transit for nine months before they finally arrived in Israel.

My father was ten years older than my mother. As a boy

he was sent very often to my grandfather's factory to buy soap, and he remembered my grandfather's youngest daughter as a two-year-old girl playing there—the little girl who much later was to become his wife.

Theirs was an arranged marriage, a Shidduch, and they had five children. All of them were born in Jerusalem.

Both of my parents, but especially my father, were very traditional without ever being fanatical. I remember all our Jewish holidays; just the preparation for them was so exciting. On Pesach we would clean the whole house, burn all the *chumetz,* all the leftover bread, and finally, for the Seder evening, we would wear our new clothes. Of course, we'd sit together the whole night for the Seder, eat, sing, and celebrate the miraculous flight of the people of Israel from Egypt, from slavery to freedom, through the reading of the Pesach Haggada.

**ENRI:** For us the holidays were not that exciting, but when I first met Mazal I was invited for the Seder. It was so different to celebrate it with the *Mizrachim,* the Jews coming from the Middle Eastern countries! It was such a nice experience. A lot of spicy and colorful food on the table, all the family was there, and they read the whole Haggada! And they really meant it! Our family did not keep the holidays as a religious ritual; a holiday was just another occasion for a festive dinner.

**MAZAL:** When I asked him what his family would do on Yom Kippur, he answered that they took the car and went to synagogue! By car on Yom Kippur!!!

We fasted on Yom Kippur and when I was little, even

when I was only nine or ten, I was already fasting with my parents and to see how far I could get. Each and every year on Yom Kippur, my father walked with us children to the Tomb of King David on Mount Zion. We wore our best white clothes and also white sports shoes.

Jerusalem was still divided then; we could not go to the Old City, just to Mount Zion, which was right at the border. When we walked there, I would often chew on *Charuvim* (carob beans) because the long walk made me very hungry. When my father saw it, he told us that we, the children, did not have to fast and that we could eat if we were hungry. We kids played on the roofs while my father prayed. And from time to time we went under his *tallit* [prayer shawl] for some prayers.

It was exciting to go to the Old City after 1967. It was like going to a very exotic place. It was so colorful; I could go there for hours and walk around. For years before the first Intifada, and then again after the peace process had started, we would go there. I remember days it was so crowded there that you almost could not pass through the narrow alleys. I don't remember feeling any fear at that time. We would sit in the cafés and restaurants, we would stroll around in the bazaar, and we would go to the Wailing Wall, and stick a little note with our wishes between the huge old stones.

After 1967, my father went there very often. On Yom Kippur, on all the High Holidays, and certainly on Tisha b'Av, the day of fasting, when we remember the destruction for the First and the Second Temple.

**ENRI:** I know a lot about our tradition and religion, but I do not like religions. I think that the religious people spoil things. For me there is a difference between the faith, your personal belief, and organized religion. A lot of things Marx said were probably wrong. But I strongly believe that religion is an opiate for the people.

**MAZAL:** We have a lot of discussions about that; I tried to instill some warm feelings for our tradition in Enri and the children. I loved my childhood in Jerusalem. I also remember the old Arab women from a neighboring Arab village, who were my mother's friends. She spoke Arabic with them and she bought vegetables and fruits that the people from the village grew. My brother-in-law, whose ancestors lived in Jerusalem for nine generations, says that there were always good relations between them and their Arab neighbors.

Years later I studied in Tel Aviv. I lived there for three years. But I missed the atmosphere in Jerusalem. I had my family here. Enri and I met in Tel Aviv, but after we got married we moved back to Jerusalem and our four children were all born here.

I wanted to teach my children about their tradition because I think it is very important. We do light the Shabbat candles very often and I am happy when my children think of it themselves and bring the candles out on Friday evenings. It is not the same as it was in my family and sometimes I feel sorry about that. When my father was still alive, we would very often spend Friday evenings with the whole big family.

**ENRI:** Even I, as a total atheist, loved that the children in my son Oded's kindergarten celebrated "Welcoming the Shabbat."

**MAZAL:** I still think we taught our children too little about our traditions. Perhaps they will discover them one day. And, hopefully, without the fanaticism you can see in many religious people around this area.

———

*Amal*
*November 7, 2002*

Dear Odelia,
I was born and raised in my homeland, Palestine. My mother told me that I was the easiest and fastest birth for her. Sometimes I seriously ask myself why I wanted to arrive so quickly into a world where I am bound by this lack of freedom. Alas, my fate is not in my hands, but in those of Allah. When I was very little, my father would work many months each year in Dubai. There we lived a very nice, beautiful life. I even remember the kids I used to play with as if it were yesterday. But most of all, I remember my mother's father. We loved each other so-o much. Grandpa told everybody that I was his favorite grandchild: He would always give me ice cream or buy me dolls.

After the Gulf War, we moved back to Jerusalem because there was no work anymore in Dubai.[1] One year later my grandpa died. Everybody was crying, except me. It made me feel awful, so I went to the kitchen, took some ice, and rubbed it into my eyes until they became all red to pretend that I had also cried. Only years later did the tears really

———

[1]Many Palestinians were forced to leave the Emirates and Kuwait after the 1991 Gulf War as a punishment for the PLO's support for Iraq's dictator, Saddam Hussein.

flow: My daddy had bought ice cream for my two little sisters and me. I was supposed to get the special one but I kept on refusing it until I finally broke down and couldn't stop sobbing. The whole episode had reminded me of my grandpa: When he bought ice cream for all his grandchildren, I would always get the special one.

After Grandpa's death, I had the feeling that my whole life had seriously changed. We did not travel to Dubai anymore. My grandmother and all my uncles had also moved from there to Jordan after the 1991 Gulf War. My Grandfather, who would take us for long walks, was no longer around. My father kept working hard to provide us with food, clothing, and shelter, and my mother became more tired because by then I had two more little sisters. Where would she take us for walks or outings? It was dangerous for her, so we preferred not to go without my father who would protect us from danger.[2] But he could only make time for us on holidays.

It was around that time when Daddy went with us to buy new clothes for our holiday *Id al-Fitr*. We took the bus and after a while this Israeli police officer entered. He came straight to my father to ask for his identity card. My father asked him: There are a lot of people on the bus; is it because I am an Arab that you ask for my identity card? The policeman with this stony face just took the paper, checked it, and handed it back without saying even one word. This was the first time that I felt that I was different. In Dubai never

---

[2]The Intifada broke out in 1987. When Amal's family came back to Jerusalem in 1991, there were still daily violent clashes between Israeli police and Palestinians in Gaza, the West Bank, and Jerusalem.

would anyone have asked my daddy for an identity card. I was only about seven years old and I wondered: What exactly does it mean to be an Arab?

When, as a little child, I saw all those scenes from the first Intifada on TV, Daddy always tried to make me understand that this would go away. Or that it wasn't real and that I shouldn't take it too seriously. He wanted me to have a happy life and not to become unhappy and depressed. Of course, he knew that he could not hide the reality from me forever. After all, I kept on asking questions. Finally, Daddy and Grandfather, my father's father, explained to me that one day the British people had ruled over Palestine and let all the Jews come in our country and that the British had given them all this land. The Palestinians fought against it, but to no avail. I was also told about massacres in Deir Yassin, which the Jews had committed. And that those massacres made many Palestinians run away in fear and despair. This is why we call the War of 1948 *Al Naqba*, the Catastrophe. My father then told me that he was about eleven years old when the Six Day War broke out. This war, Daddy told me, the Arabs call *Al Naqse*, the Defeat. Daddy told me that to him it was also like the Catastrophe, because instead of getting the land that was taken by the Jews in 1948, the Arabs lost the rest, too. This is how we came under Israeli rule. When Daddy told me all this at the around the end of the First Intifada, he said, "It is not just fiction, what you have seen on television. It is reality."

It is strange, though: I understood that two peoples were fighting for one land and that our land had been taken away from us. But I still did not really grasp the reality around me. I remember that when Daddy would go shopping in

Ramallah, he would ask us kids, "Which of you wants to come with me?" and we'd all scream, "Me! Me!" and fight to accompany him. Why? Because we thought we would make a little trip abroad. Ramallah or Bethlehem or any other place in the West Bank seemed like another country to me because there were soldiers and checkpoints when we crossed the "border" into those "foreign lands." One day Daddy told us that it was not really another country, even if there were checkpoints. It still did not occur to me to ask questions like: Why is it that both we and they "over there" in Ramallah are Palestinians? Or why is there a checkpoint between here and there if we are one people? I did not care that much, but rather wished to play with other kids.

I don't remember much about the peace process. Not the signing of the treaty in Washington or Yassir Arafat returning to Gaza. I was only nine years old then. For some reason, I do remember the opening of the Palestinian airport in Gaza. And, of course, I remember that we could do our shopping freely in Ramallah and go there five times a day if we wanted to.

When there was peace and quiet, I basically forgot about the whole situation and just wanted to do "normal stuff." I really only paid attention to the political situation when negative stuff started happening again. For example, when Itzchak Rabin was killed because he wanted peace. I saw it on TV and my whole family talked about his assassination. When Daddy watches the news, the whole family watches with him. He explained to me that Rabin wanted peace and that this was exactly why he was killed. Now I can't erase this thought from my mind: Somebody wanted to right a wrong, somebody wanted to do justice for people, and he had to die for it.

My whole life I only wanted to be left alone and just live my life with my family. When I started to meet those people from *Peace Child Israel,* I also had to learn about the others. So only over the last two or three years have I begun to study more of our most recent history. Politics sometimes makes my head spin; I get a headache from it. It sometimes makes me crazy to think that when the Jews began to come, the Arabs had much more land than the Jews and now it is exactly the other way around. It makes me angry! I thought that even the partition plan in 1947 was unfair. What right did the Jews have to take the land so that we would be forced to share it with them? They were only successful because the British helped them with the Balfour Declaration when they promised them the Jewish homeland.

I prefer not to think about that. I would like to think about the future; I would just like to think about what I will be doing with my life. But since this war keeps going on all the time, I cannot forget it and the past makes me angry again.

My grandfather who went through all this is not that angry anymore, even though he saw with his very own eyes what had happened. He is old and just doesn't want to be angry anymore. I wrote down a conversation I had with him about his life. I would like you to read it.

Amal

*Amal's Grandfather Tells His Story*

We Palestinians were unlucky. Before the British came here in the First World War, the Turks ruled this part of the world.

Once upon a time the Arabs were educated. Al Andalus, Granada, the Muslim empire in southern Spain—all are proof of that. But throughout the five-hundred years that the Turks governed the Near East, there was not even one new school or university opened. Therefore, people were very simple, uneducated, and not really ready for a war. The Jews who came were much more sophisticated and much smarter.

I married in 1943, when I was only sixteen. My father wanted me to marry, even though I was so young. From then on I had to support a wife and then a family. Young people don't know anymore what it means to be married and to have to support a family at so young an age.

At that time the Second World War was on and I found myself a job with the British army. Their headquarters for the whole Middle East was close to Beersheva. Of course, they had a very large canteen and a very big gas station for some twenty thousand vehicles. I was smart enough to be hired to do the shopping for the canteen. I also was on night-shift very often. Most of the time, I guarded the gas station. Gasoline was in short supply during the war and I had to make sure that nobody stole the gasoline. I kept myself awake by burning wood into charcoal, painting a moustache on my face, and washing it off again. I was so young, I didn't yet have a real moustache.

I worked with the British until they left in 1948. I was lucky. I didn't go to college or high school or anything. We Muslims believe God gives to you when you work hard. Things don't come in your sleep. I was working very hard, and I guess I was also smart, even without a proper education.

Before the war in 1948, the Jews wouldn't dare enter our village. During the war there were fierce battles going on around Jerusalem. Since the railway line, which was important to both Jews and Arabs, also ran through our village, I also expected battles there. Therefore, I moved my family to safety in Ramallah, where there was not much fighting going on.

At the end it was not fighting, but probably some secret negotiations that decided the fate of our village. Some of the Jewish officers in the Israeli army, among them Moshe Dayan, were negotiating a cease-fire. So, they had to meet some officers of the Jordanian Arab League and the *Mukhtar* [Mayor] with a delegation from our village. I was also supposed to be part of this delegation. At the agreed-upon time, we, the people from the village, tried to get to the meeting point in our village, but there was heavy fighting going on. Nobody was killed, but we all ran away. When we came the next morning, the new "borders" were already clear. There were fences between us and the next village. Families were split apart. Fortunately, our people didn't leave their village, as many other Palestinians had who fled from their homes.

After the war, the refugees came and were put in different camps, like Kalandia near Ramallah or Aida and Daheishe near Bethlehem. I worked in the refugee camps; helping register the refugees. I helped with everything, I knew about organization. A Red Cross officer came and asked me how much money I got for my work. I told him that I did it voluntarily and lived and supported my family on my savings. He hired me for nine dinars a month. That was a lot of money at the time. My younger brother helped me line up the people for food and water. He was also hired for a little less money. Then I even got a raise from the Red Cross. Again, I was lucky. Most of my friends didn't have jobs, but I was an employee of the Red Cross.

When the Red Cross handed over the refugee camps to the UN Work and Relief Agency (UNWRA) on May 1, 1950, there was no job for me anymore. They didn't need so many people. But I knew a few boys from the village who had gone to Dubai after the war. They helped me to get a visa and I moved my wife and the children to Dubai in 1952. Again, I was working with some British company there, which maintained all sorts of infrastructure projects: schools, desalination plants. There was nothing in Dubai at the time. Let alone air-conditioning. It was unbearably hot. Every morning, when the workers moved from their living quarters to the factories, it looked like a big army moving toward the desert. I liked working with the British. Those people were OK, even though I didn't like the politics of their government. I mean, wasn't it scandalous to bring all those Jews into our land?

Once a year I came for a visit to Jerusalem. It was hard. For the first time, I had to leave my family—my parents, sisters, and brothers. One part of the family lived under Jordanian rule, after Jordan had taken over the West Bank and the eastern part of Jerusalem. The other part had ended up in Israel, because they had married somebody from the neighboring village and moved there shortly before it was conquered by the Jews. Also, my mother-in-law lived in Israel, on the other side of the fence that had become our new border. We couldn't have contact with them. And it was so close. We could see them from our village, see them moving around, see them working in the fields, but we were not allowed to talk to them. Both sides would put you in jail for making contact. One day one of my sisters-in-law living under Jordanian rule tried to make contact with her mother. The Jordanians put her in jail for a whole year.

After four years in Dubai, I came back home. It was too hard for me—the working conditions, the heat, the separation from the family. Then one of my brothers decided that he wanted to study in America. My job here at home paid just enough to support my wife and children. But in our tradition you support whomever needs it. I thought it would be better to go back to Dubai again, because I could earn much more money there in order to support my brother's studies. In 1957, I went back and got almost the same job again. I was in charge of the guesthouse in a British housing project. But in 1966, I returned to Palestine. Just one year before the Israelis conquered us.

Actually, I didn't see much war going on. It all happened so fast. I owned an Opel Rekord at the time, one of four cars in our village. So I went back and forth between here and Ramallah, where I had put the kids with some other family. When I came back to our village, there were Israeli soldiers all over the place. In Ramallah the people were afraid. A friend of mine was panicky and asked me: Shall we run away? Perhaps they do bad things to the women, perhaps there will be massacres as in some Arab villages during the war in 1948. In Ramallah I met a priest from the Anglican church and asked him what to do. He comforted me and said: I don't think the Israeli army will do anything to the people. But still, my friend fled. He is still outside, poor guy.

We really had a hard time, we Palestinians. The land my family owned was lost in 1948. It would have been worth millions by now. After 1967, an Israeli came and wanted to buy some of it. He had seen my title to it in the books. I told him he could have one dunum for free; he would just have to settle the deal with the Israeli authorities. He came back to me and said: You did not tell me the land was sold already! Well, actually I did not sell it. They took it away, and it was declared state land. Compensation? No way. People said one day there would be a settlement and then we would get compensation for what has been lost. But probably my great-great grandchildren will not even see it. My grandchildren are losing their feeling for what had belonged to us, for our land and our home. They don't know where exactly the land was. They don't feel it with their hearts.

When I was working with the British during the Second World War, of course, we heard some of the news. We heard what had been done to the Jews in Europe and I thought it was horrible. We also had heard about the promise the British gave to the Jews, to build a homeland for them in Palestine. But we didn't think it would go this way. And our own leaders? What could they do? They didn't have the money, the means. They are lacking sophistication. And the other Arab leaders simply did not care. Abdel Khader al Husseini, one of our few good leaders, went to Syria before the war in 1948 to ask for money, arms, and support. He came back empty-handed but with lots of promises: The Arab armies would come to liberate Palestine. They really came—the Egyptians, the Jordanians, the Syrians. The Iraqis and the Lebanese, too. Well, instead of taking back our land, the Arab armies lost even more. And the Jews weren't even that strong at the time; they didn't have such a highly equipped army as they do now.

Our war is really different from other wars. I think the Jews have a right to live and have a place for themselves. But what about us? Where is the justice? Is it fair to bring somebody else and throw me out?

But *Hamdullilah,* praise Allah, we are still alive.

# Seven

## SCHOOL

*Amal*
*October 19, 2002*

Dear Odelia,

I was at first flabbergasted when I started to work at this
Jewish-Arab school. My girlfriend, who had worked there
before me and introduced me to the headmaster of this
school, told me that it was different. That the teachers there
have the goal of forming strong personalities. And that they
want to develop tolerance between Arabs and Jews. But in
the first couple of days, those kids really amazed me. They
don't raise their hands to ask whether they can leave the
room. I mean, really, the fact that they just came and went
as they pleased drove me crazy. When I told one of the kids
that he should be a bit more quiet and that he can't just
leave the room, he answered me back: "How is that your
business? You are not the teacher anyway; you are only the
teacher's aide." Or when I asked kids to come back into class
after recess because I would have liked to start playing or
painting with the group, they looked at me as if I were speaking Chinese, and they stayed where they were. When I told

them that I would inform the teachers, they snapped back at me: "We don't care!" I think these kids are not developing strong personalities; they are developing rude personalities.

Later, I changed my mind a bit. I really love all those kids in the class. Things are much better now, much more disciplined. The kids respect me. Nobody tells me anymore, "That's not your business" when I ask them to do something. If nothing else works, I threaten to tell the headmistress. She is a very tough Arabic woman. Everybody is afraid of her.

There are also very nice kids in the school who ask very politely for permission to go to the bathroom. But I do understand that there is really a big difference in our cultures.

In the school I attended, it was impossible to just leave the classroom without asking permission first. If you did that, you would be kicked out. When the teacher asked for quiet, there would be quiet. Of course, there were also rude boys who would keep on chattering all the time. But when the teacher said something, his word counted and the students obeyed. In our tradition, you learn from your parents and in school to be very respectful toward your elders. You don't raise your voice when speaking to them, you definitely don't use impolite or rude words, and if an older person tells you something, you have to respect it, because he is old and knows better than you do. Never shout at adults. If I disagreed with somebody about something—doesn't matter if it was my parents or the teachers at school—I would put it very politely. I never would have told an older person "This is not business." Never in my life, neither at school or at home, did I use the expression "I don't care" when I was told something. That's unthinkable, and I am pretty flabbergasted about how easily kids use that in that school. If I thought I was right and the elders were wrong, I would speak up very politely or not at all.

OK, I understand that the kids are definitely quiet when they have "real" class. But still they should treat every person in authority, everyone who is older, with respect. In our school, all the students could also voice their opinion, but they would do it very politely. But overall, there was real discipline in our school, which I really liked.

Yours,
Amal

*Odelia*
*October 21, 2002*

Dear Amal,

Well, the kids were cheeky and not polite, did not obey you or didn't listen to what you said. It's funny, because it really says something about our different mentalities. Kids wouldn't behave like that in all the Israeli schools, but in my school we didn't have to sit up straight, raise our hands in order to ask permission to go to the bathroom, or be so utterly polite all the time. During the last year at school, we didn't even come to school regularly. We'd just come for the tests and basically study at home for our exams. Or not. Well, I learned a bit. After all, I passed the Bagrut with considerably good grades, but it wasn't such a big thing.

I think it is quite peculiar: For most of the Arab kids I know, it was such a big deal to pass with good grades. All of them were very tense: We have to get really good grades, we really have to learn and study hard. It was so important to them. For me it wasn't that important. I just wanted to have that Bagrut certificate with some grade on it. I, and most of my friends, didn't care about the marks. Of course, there were some really ambitious students and there were people who cried because they didn't get excellent marks.

But in general it is less formal in our schools: You don't have school uniforms as in Arab schools. I talked with my friends from the *kommuna* in Kfar Saba about our schools. We all agreed that it was not very formal in Israeli schools. Basically, they give you a choice. If you want to learn, you learn. If not, OK, then you go can home. That's how it goes. I like what Mark Twain said about school: "I never let school interfere with my education." I think education should not be to stand up in school or listen to everything the teacher says and write it down as if these were holy words. At my school it was actually very interesting sometimes. We had lively political discussions and occasional fights. They were pretty liberal. You could criticize, say what you wanted, argue with your teachers. At the end of the year, and especially for us twelfth-graders who were about to leave school after the Bagrut exams anyway, everything was a bit more loose. Some of the students actually came to school, sat on the stairs to the entrance, and smoked cigarettes. That meant nothing. We were good kids, we just wanted to show: Ha, ha, we have finished all our tests and we are leaving school for summer vacation or really forever and now we will smoke in your faces. The teachers didn't care. They knew that we were good kids, they knew that we were not under their authority anymore and that we just wanted to let loose and probably show off a bit. We wanted that one moment of freedom and a little rebellion, too.

It's obviously so different from what you experienced. It

seems so strange to me that in your school, kids were thrown out if they did not behave respectfully enough toward the teacher. Well, there might be some schools like that in Israel, but most schools I know let the kids do what they want. They are giving them freedom because, in the end, the kids are going to learn and to work well in class. But most Israeli kids want to go to school because all their friends go. Kids are constantly asked: Which grade are you in? And if a kid would have to admit that he dropped out, everybody would be shocked. There are a lot of things I really don't like about school. But most of all it teaches you one good thing: It educates you about how to deal with people. Even with stupid, spineless people like some teachers. You learn to deal with people who think they are the smartest people in the world but actually they are not. Also, how to gain confidence and learn to confront those adults who actually think that they are so much smarter than you are only because they are grown up. Or who tell you things that make absolutely no sense. And then you have some extracurricular activities like theater, which I loved s-o-o-o-o much and thought was s-o-o-o interesting. Mostly, the teachers trust the kids, trust that they would not skip classes and that would learn properly without pressure because they are interested in the stuff they are studying.

Besides, you also learn some facts such as what the Jews of Albuquerque did on February 1, 1968. No, I am making this up. We really learned every little bit about Jewish history. I guess school did not interfere too much with my education. After all, I also learned some useful stuff.

Best,

Odelia

# Eight

## THE ARMY

*Odelia*
*October 18, 2002*

Dear Amal,
You are worried how our friendship will be affected once I
will do my army service. I would like to explain some things
to you.

Army is a must; it's the law. When you are eighteen, when
you have finished high school, you have to go to the army.
Today there are lots of people who refuse, as conscientious
objectors. It is not so easy to get out, because you have to
write letters and justify the reasons that you don't want to
do your service, or you might get out on medical reasons.
But in general, it's obligatory. Because it's a must in this
country, everybody also asks you what you have done in the
army when you, for example, apply for a job. If you refuse,
you sometimes have problems in the future because people
always ask what you have done. On the other hand, the army
also opens up opportunities. Kids, for example, who did not
do that well in school and, therefore, don't have a very bright
future ahead of them can take their Bagrut exam focusing

عريقات: طالبنا واشنطن بوضع آلية تنفيذ وجدول زمني لإقامة الدولة

# وفد فلسطيني يجري محادثات معمقة
# مع رايس وباول في العاصمة الأميركية

Al Hayat, August 9, 2002
Visit in Washington
**Subhead:** Friendly Talks Between Palestinian Delegation and U.S. Foreign
Minister Colin Powell

on the educational institutions of the army. They could still specialize in something in the army or even become a commander. After they have finished their service, they would have a much better start for their professional lives even without a good high school degree.

I think it is really complicated. Because the army descends on eighteen-year-old kids, and we are just kids, and tells them: From now on you are a soldier. You cut your hair, shave, look nice, take your piercings off, and start acting like a soldier. Two minutes before, you were a teenage high school kid and now you are suddenly a soldier. Take this gun, learn how to use it, but don't just use it without thinking, because, after all, it's a gun; it can take lives. So be careful, be moral, good luck. What?

Of course, we have all these preparation courses in school and army people are invited to lecture us. You might have heard from all these people preparing you at school, you heard the army slang from older friends, you heard the stories from your parents who were also in the army and therefore they assume that we "know" a lot. But still it is not the same when you are actually in it. When you are in it yourself, it is scary. I mean, you give the kid a gun, and he is not only practicing with it. And he also might die and he is probably only twenty years old, which means he still is a kid who didn't have much of a chance to live his life.

We shouldn't make the kids go into the army right after school. But then: Who would join the army? The older guys who want to go university, or the much older adults who want to start families? That's also a much-debated issue. Is it right to take kids after school and send them to the army? Maybe we should send people who are a bit older, but they have already started a life. It is complex, very complex.

In a war like this, it is difficult to make decisions. What if you are standing at a barrier or you get an order not to let anybody out of the Occupied Territories, and an ambulance needs to get through? But no people—yes, also no ambulances, because it happened that there were suicide bombers in ambulances. This is why they check everybody. And there is just a kid at a barrier and he has gotten this order, and he is in a situation where he has to play God. Is this person in the ambulance out to kill me or is he gravely sick and on his way to the hospital? This is a serious issue: How do you respond to it? What if you let it through and it is your fault that somebody blows himself up and kills many people? It is not as easy as it looks on television. It is really easy to take the big conqueror, the occupier, the ruler, and blame him for everything, as I see the army represented on foreign news stations. Or to use this phrase for the army: a "well-oiled military machine." Yes, it is well-oiled machinery and merely thinking about that gives me the creeps sometimes. But you

הסי.איי.אי הציג תוכנית חדשה לרפורמות ברשות הפלשתינאית

Haaretz, August 9, 2002
CIA Presents New Plan for Reforms in Palestinian Authority

have to understand: Essentially, it is built by human beings. From this and that kid and this kid. And I know they are kids, because now that I am at that age, I walk down the streets and I see friends of mine who are in the army.

The other day I got off the bus in Jerusalem and ran into this friend from school. She was in her uniform and she had a huge rifle with her. She was a fighter. I greeted her, of course, and I hugged her, but I thought: Oh God, she is part of that "well-oiled military machine," and she had a huge rifle slung over her shoulder. Only a month ago, she was sitting in my class, and I know she is a great person. And I know she's going to do OK; she will try to act as morally as possible. But sometimes this idea of your friends becoming soldiers is just incomprehensible to me. I mean, I am used to seeing male soldiers and women soldiers, even those fighting, and this is how things go. I always had something against the army, because the whole institution was frightening for a kid. But now these are my friends in the army and I understand that it is not abstract. It is built by people who also happen to be my friends. That's what people from the outside don't see.

When the Intifada began, I didn't really think about what it would mean for my life. Now it has gotten so close. When we were younger, our parents used to tell us: "Don't worry, when you grow up, you won't have to go to the army." All parents in Israel say that to their kids because they believed that by then, there would be peace. A few weeks ago, I was sitting together with some friends of mine. All of them had just finished high school, and all of them had gotten their call for the army. And we started making jokes. Oh yeah, right, didn't our parents tell us that we wouldn't have to go to the army when we grew up?

Most of my friends are in the army now, a few of them in fighting units. It really scares me. I am afraid that one day I will be watching the news and see the little photo of a friend of mine with a candle next to it and they'll say that he is gone. "It is likely to happen.

We did not choose to fight. I mean, the kids who go into the army did not choose to fight. They can refuse, but some people like me do not want to refuse. It will be interesting to see how the army works. I sometimes have deep arguments with my friends, as I did at this birthday party once. As we were sitting and drinking beer, someone in the group said: "It is stupid not to go to the army and not to enlist, as some people do now, because it won't change a thing. The only way to change things is from within the army. From within the system." They said that if you were outside the system you didn't matter at all anymore and you couldn't change a thing. Some claimed that only by refusing your obligatory service, or by refusing further [obligatory] service as a reservist, could you have an effect because this gets media attention; they would listen to us. One guy said: "Listen, I know that I can make a difference and change a lot by the way I behave when I am on duty. According to the law, I have the right to refuse orders if I consider them immoral. If you refuse the entire service on grounds that you are a conscientious objector—the army just lets you go and that's it. But I plan to make a difference by the way I behave in the army."

To go to the army is not that big a thing in Israel. It is part of everybody's life. Most of the people in the world go through a sequence of kindergarten, school, university, family. In Israel it is very much the same, except between school and university there is the army. People see it as a part of their life that they have just to get over with.

Since the army is obligatory, I think that makes the army more moral. Well, I know "army" and "moral" seem to be a contradiction in terms. After all, an army is a fighting machine. I think our army is more moral than other armies in the world because the kids did not choose to go there. If the situation were different and the army service was not obligatory, most kids would not go the army voluntarily, I think. We are tired of all this fighting. But then the only people to go to the army would be the hard-liners, or even racists and crazies, who really want to fight and to kill. Then the army would be like the armies in most places all over the world. That would be frightening.

Ruthi, one of my friends in *HaShomer HaZair,* who lives with me in this *kommuna,* is going to a fighting unit. We asked her why she was doing it, why she would join the army and, above all, a fighting unit? She said, "I prefer that I am the one standing at a barrier instead of a right-wing fascist standing there." I think she has a point. That's the reason that many people, who are really against fighting, still do their army service, do the hard staff, and are forced to make some tough choices. They want to balance it. They are liberal and more open and certainly they don't want to kill. When they stand guard at a barrier, they are not going to play the tough guy and think they can kick everybody around, because they will try to remain moral people and bring their attitude and their moral point of view to the job.

Why am I going into the army? I never really wanted to and my father supported me in that. He thinks that I would just be wasting my time. But when I thought more about it, I realized that the army experience is such a big part of Israeli life. It's something so big that I really want to understand it; I want to understand what it is like to be part of that "well-oiled machine." Right now I am criticizing what I see from the outside or what I see on television. But I don't see it all, really, neither the bad, nor the good. You don't really see the bloodshed that is going on. On the other hand, we don't really see the reasons for all that and we forget that there are also many good, moral people in the army. How would I know that? Because some of them are my friends, people I have known for a long time.

I did say no to a couple of things about my army service. I don't want to be in a fighting unit; that's for sure. And if I had to be a fighter, I definitely would not go into the Occupied Territories. Neither would I like to protect the Jewish settlements in those Territories. I don't want to serve in a unit where I have to make really tough choices about life and death. Try to imagine, for example, that an agent from the Intelligence Services got information that a suicide bomber was hiding in a particular house. He knew that for sure. But he also knew that with him there was a family of twelve kids, for instance. So what are you going to do? If you don't kill this guy right now, you are failing to prevent a terrorist attack that might also kill many children. But if you pass on the information, a bomb could be thrown right into this house, which could kill twelve kids along with the suicide bomber. I don't want to face those issues; I would not like to make decisions like that or even think about them. I don't want to make the wrong choices or play God.

What I want to do in the army is participate in the education program. In the army there are language-training programs for new immigrants and schools for people who dropped out of high school and want to have a second chance to pass their Bagrut exam.

I am just trying to offer a different point of view from what people abroad usually think about the army. What I am saying that it is not that bad and that other armies probably are much worse. Yes, I am absolutely aware that awful things happen. We probably don't even know the half of it or the reasons behind it, and I don't think that the media really informs us about it. No doubt there are certainly some idiots in the army who try to be macho and do awful things.

Things are much more complicated than they seem. What the media shows us is never altogether true, objective, or the whole picture. From neither side do you get the whole picture, not from yours, Amal, not from mine, and not from an outsider's point of view. The army is not only a machine that can be horrible. It is made up of individuals. And I do believe it could be more horrible if it were the army of a different country. I understood this so much better when, all of a sudden, my friends were part of that fighting machine. Most of them know how to deal with difficult issues, or so I hope. Most of them try to maintain their morals and won't act mean if somebody wants to pass by a barrier. They would

be the ones who would counterbalance the extremists.
Yours,
Odelia

*Amal*
*November 5, 2002*

Dear Odelia,
There is really not much that I can say about you being in
the army. You tell me that you want to act responsibly in the
army and that you don't want to serve in a fighting unit or
in the Occupied Territories. That's completely your choice
and not mine. I just think: Why do you have to be in the
army at all? I mean, you can also act responsibly if you are
*not* in the army!

What can I say about it? I still know that I will have difficulties seeing you in an Israeli army uniform. I don't know
why everybody has to go into the army and why there is this
need for a strong army all the time. Unlike you, we don't
have an army, which makes the whole thing so unfair. And
the Arab leaders are weak and only care about themselves.
They only have big mouths and there is nothing behind what
they say.
Amal

## Nine

## HOW I BECAME WHAT I AM

*Odelia*
*November 2002*

Dear Amal,
I thought a lot about the question "What made me the person I am?" I think that my parents taught me to think independently. Of course, they teach you what's good and bad, right and wrong, but in my opinion a lot of freedom was given to me. Not too much to make me feel completely disconnected and not know what to do. I told my mother that she was pretty good at educating kids.

My movement also helped me understand many new things a lot. The people from *Shomer HaZair* always came to our school. It used to be a school that was loosely affiliated with the Labor movement. I went to *Shomer HaZair* because of my friends and because I thought it was interesting. I did not really understand the political implications at first. Only during the last year did I delve more deeply into all those questions: What is capitalism? What is socialism? What does it mean? I only rarely had discussions with my father who also was in a socialist-Zionist movement when he was young. I guess I was too young and too busy being a teenager. My mother says that, politically, my ideas are very close to my father's but we did not talk that much about politics. Maybe there is a socialist-Zionist gene?

I guess that all of them, my parents, my friends, and the people from my movement helped me to become a person who is more open-minded. I try not to form an opinion right away but to understand what's going on first.

An attitude of "always criticize, always look twice, and never accept things as they appear in the first place" probably makes you a mensch—a decent and compassionate human being. Don't just swallow everything they tell you. Look at the world, smile, because that makes things easier, but always with a question mark. And always ask yourself: Why is that so? Why am I supposed to do things this or that way? Is what I am told true? This examining, nonstop examining, is something that really characterizes me and I love it. I really think that one person can make things better. Like let's go do community service with fourteen other kids and live in a big house and have a lot of fun. Cool! I am doing something with my life; I am affecting kids in a positive way! Next year I will be in the army, doing nothing useful there, yeah! Just kidding. Maybe I can find some area where I can have a positive influence. And after that, I would like to make my dream come true and just: *Live!*

Odelia

*Amal*
*November 2002*

Dear Odelia,

All my life, my daddy has had the biggest impact on me. I respect him so very much. There are a lot of families in which the father never has time for his children. It was totally different in my family. My parents love each other very much and we all grew up in an environment of trust and love. My parents, especially my daddy, always had time for us, no matter how busy he might have been. He always had the patience to answer all our questions. And he trusts me completely. In our tradition, it is not common to let a girl travel in a group with other young kids, especially kids who have a totally different background, to some foreign place. But my father let me travel to Switzerland because he knew that he could trust me a hundred percent.

I believe that I basically formed my opinions from the experiences I have had in daily life and from the news on TV. It was quite common in our family that my father would watch the news—and he watched all news channels like Al-Jazeera or Abu Dhabi news, sometimes even the news on Israeli TV—and explained everything we did not understand, especially when we were much younger.

When it came to questions about our traditions and religion, about love and marriage, or when I had any sorts of problems, I would always turn to my older sister. She really has had a strong influence on me. She is so patient. She never got mad at me when I made a mistake, but rather tried to find some solution without creating too much of a stir. She was also the one who introduced me to my fiancé.

In Switzerland, some people asked me where I came from and when I said that I was from Palestine, they didn't understand. So I corrected myself and said, "From Israel." It hurt me, since I am not an Israeli. I would like to be able one day to pull out my own Palestinian passport at a border crossing and to answer the question about where I came from proudly with "From Palestine."
Amal

# AFTERWORD

In this second Intifada more than a quarter of the casualties on both sides are people under twenty years old. Young Israelis and Palestinians are growing up in an atmosphere of hatred and violence. It would not be surprising, therefore, if they perceived the other side only as the "Enemy" and that any attempt to find a compromise with this frightening "other" would be futile.

When Amal and Odelia began working on this book, they had just left their formative childhood years behind and had become two very strong personalities with equally strong ideals and values. Neither Amal nor Odelia believed that the Israeli-Palestinian conflict could ever be solved by violence. In the course of writing this book, not only did they explore the other's positions, but also their own. I invited them to reflect on the question of what had shaped their adult personalities. I also wanted them to consider the future. A conversation between the three of us seemed to be the right forum to deliberate on the challenges for the continuation of their friendship in an increasingly violent environment. But we also strongly felt that we should end this book with a vivid expression of what Amal and Odelia had achieved,

*something needed so badly in that part of the world: a dia-
logue across cultural and political barriers.*

*November 15, 2002*

**ODELIA:** You know, the most interesting thing about doing
this book was that I found out a lot of things about myself.
I've never talked much about politics or the conflict. I never
knew that I had all those thoughts and ideas about it until I
sat down and really thought about it.

**AMAL:** I feel the same way.

**ODELIA:** Usually we avoid those things because they are difficult and you don't really want to think about it.

**AMAL:** Yes, and if you want to build a friendship, then you
have to skip the political thing—at least in the beginning—
because it is very difficult to accept somebody else's opinion
on such emotional matters.

**ODELIA:** When you live in this situation, it is often too difficult
to face it, because you just want to live your life like everybody else. And the worlds we live in are so different. Very
often, we just don't want to make the effort to get to know
someone whose background is so different from our own.
Besides, you already have friends from your own world, so
you don't bother that much.

**AMAL:** Every time we hear the news and learn that, again,
there was some attack or fighting or a bomb dropped in Gaza

and that people got killed, it would seriously affect the friendship between an Israeli and an Arab, I guess. They would immediately talk about politics and get into an argument. Politics could destroy everything here.

**ODELIA:** But I also think that friendship is not possible without talking about politics when you have this kind of situation. It influences our daily lives even we don't want it to. I can also see this from the friends I have: They mostly have the same views as I do. It is really almost impossible to connect with people who don't think alike. I would find it hard to connect with someone from the settlements, for instances. Someone who is really right wing. I would feel too different from him. Our basic values and world views would be too different, and I could not accept that.

**AMAL:** I think the same thing. I also could not connect with somebody, even an Arab, if he or she had totally different ideas. It certainly would then be easier to become friends with somebody Jewish, even though she came from a different world.

**ODELIA:** Even though we probably never would have met without organizations like *Peace Child Israel*, because the basic things we do are not the same. We don't go to the same places, even though we live so close to each other.

**AMAL:** Yes, we are living totally different lives. We do not go to the same schools. My culture, my religion is different.

**ODELIA:** We aren't talking about the same things even when we talk about the same topic, like boyfriends, for instance. There is a big gap between what I am allowed to do and what you are allowed to do.

**AMAL:** Yes. I can only talk to boys; that's it.

**ODELIA:** And there is a big gap between our points of view on different things in both of our societies. We have different ways of looking at things.

**SYLKE TEMPEL:** Do you realize that in the beginning you were almost shy with one another and only later you dared to criticize each other's views more harshly?

**ODELIA:** That's natural. When you have a close friend, you can tell her everything. From little things like "I don't like your new hairstyle" to "I don't agree with your opinions about this and that." I think if we could keep up this friendship for a long time, then we would become really very good friends. But this friendship is a lot more difficult than one I would have with people from my own background. It is both politics and our different circumstances in life that make it harder.

**AMAL:** Of course. When I criticize a good friend, she will not be mad at me because she knows and respects me. What will happen, though, when you go to the army and I cannot connect with you? Then it will be very difficult to continue our friendship.

**ODELIA**: I understand that it is very hard to see me in the army while the army is your enemy.

**AMAL**: We will just have such different lives. You will go into the army, and I will get married, but whatever happens I will not forget that you were somebody I knew and exchanged all those letters with.

**ODELIA**: If you write a book together and you basically get to know about each other's lives, then, of course, you develop a much better connection. But it is still difficult.

**AMAL**: Even if we lose contact again, there is something between us now and we would always connect with each other, even if we only met each other by accident in the street.

**ST**: What was the most surprising thing you heard about the other?

**ODELIA**: The marriage. I first thought it would be impossible for me to understand why an eighteen-year-old girl would want to get married. Now I am really happy for you because you explained your traditions and you are continuing with your education. I understand much better now. I am just not used to seeing that in my society. But I learned that it's still no reason for not doing it.

**AMAL**: I understood much better why it was important for you and people in Israel in general to go into the army. I always thought that everyone who goes to the army just wants to fight and kill the Arabs. When you explained that you really didn't want to go to a fighting unit and that you really will try hard to be a responsible person, I began to think about you and the army much differently.

**ODELIA:** I never felt that there were moments when I just could not carry on any longer with our letter writing. After all, I was prepared for the fact that we have different perspectives.

**AMAL:** I sometimes thought it was unbearable that Israelis don't know anything about our culture and we know so much more about theirs. That made me so angry.

**ODELIA:** Me, too! I guess we have to accept that there will always be different versions of the same history. And that, for that matter, there are two peoples here who will just have to live together. Or we have to kill each other which, I guess, is not really an option.

**ST:** Amal, you said that you don't really want to know about the ancient history of the Jews in Israel/Palestine. Don't you think you should know a bit more about Jewish culture and history in this part of the world and about the Jews' connection with this country, too?

**AMAL:** Well, I also think that Israel is here to stay. They didn't disappear in the last fifty years. Yes, we both have to learn about each other and to understand more about each other's cultures.

**ODELIA:** See, Jewish history and perhaps even the religion and our connection with this land might not mean that much to me anymore. I just feel at home here because I was born and raised here. But it meant, for example, a lot to my grandfather. I still don't know much about your family and your family's history, except the story your grandfather told. Or about Muslim history here in general. But I think that you should also learn that Jews came here, because they did have a connection to the land. When my mother's grandfather, who was a rabbi, came here and saw Jerusalem for the first time, he knelt down and kissed the ground. He had never been here before and he did not know what it was like. But each year at Pesach he said, as every Jew in the world does and has done for centuries: *Next year in Jerusalem.*

**AMAL:** But didn't the Zionists also want to go to other places like Uganda or Argentina? Was there also a connection with those places? Why would they come here?

**ODELIA:** They considered Uganda or Argentina for political reasons, as far as I know. They thought they could buy some land there. But then it was decided that it had to be here, because the Jews had a historical connection with this land. Everything that happened in the Bible happened here. There are lots of sites here that are holy to three religions: Islam, Christianity, and Judaism. Which everybody should understand. But certainly there is a connection between the Jews and the land. It still does not perhaps justify how everything was done. But one cannot deny the connection.

**AMAL:** There is the Church of the Nativity in Bethlehem, there is the Church of the Holy Sepulchre in Jerusalem. What if the Christians wanted to come here and take over the land because there was some Christian connection? If everybody takes the places they have a connection with, it would cause a lot of turmoil. To me, it is still unbelievable that it was possible to take the land from the Palestinians in 1948.

**ODELIA:** The fact that the Jews thought they needed a country of their own was also because of the anti-Semitism in Europe, which became even worse during the Holocaust. Perhaps they could have chosen some other place. But then there was this strong connection here on the grounds of the Bible. This was the Holy Land for the Jews. I also have a problem with how things happened, and that we have all those wars in our history.

**AMAL:** When I went to Jordan last summer, the storeowner realized that I spoke with a Palestinian accent. He told me that he was from Jaffa [near Tel Aviv] and that his grandfather had fled there in 1948. It was unbearable to me.

**ST:** There were and are, unfortunately, many refugees all over the world. And unfortunately, they have to resettle somehow and start a new life. Isn't it time for the Palestinians to move on?

**AMAL:** But people miss their homes! They have heard all the stories about their hometowns and villages from their grandparents! This man from Jaffa who spoke to me never saw the place, but it is still important to him because his ancestors were born there! Nobody can forget that!

**ST:** In the West we basically think that the conflict is about the territory that was occupied in 1967—the West Bank, Gaza, and East Jerusalem. But most of the time, you refer back to the establishment of Israel in 1948.

**AMAL:** In 1948, the British, who were a colonial power and who were only here to guard their own interests, dared to give land that did not even belong to them to somebody else, and nobody among my people would have ever dreamt in their worst nightmares that this would happen. The original refugees—plus their children and their grandchildren who are still in camps—are refugees from 1948. Also, the War of 1967 and what happened then makes me angry because that was when the other half of our land was taken away. But it was the Arab leaders' fault. Emotionally, it does not affect me as deeply as what happened in 1948.

**ST:** The issues surrounding the War of 1967 can be addressed if Israel would return the Occupied Territories. The injustice you feel was done to the Palestinians in 1948 cannot be corrected because it would mean the destruction of Israel. How do you deal with that?

**AMAL:** We have been fighting for fifty years, thousands of people have been killed, and nothing has changed. I said a thousand times that I just want to live a happy life in peace and quiet and that I am tired of all this bloodshed. We gave up all dreams of getting all of Palestine back anyway. We just finally want to have our own state where we can do whatever we want.

**ODELIA:** I understand your anger; I think it's justified. But we cannot forget about reality. We are here and have a state. And not so far into the future, you will have your state, too. I am sure about that. We are not going to disappear and you aren't either. I think neither Israelis nor Palestinians should forget the suffering inflicted on them by the other. It is important to remember history. But I also feel that Israelis and Palestinians should stop blaming one another constantly.

**AMAL:** Once the Palestinians have a real life, once we have our state and have the same opportunities as the Israelis, I am sure that our anger will fade away.

# CHRONOLOGY:
## MIDDLE EAST CONFLICT

**1881** Beginning of an organized Russian-Jewish immigration into Palestine after intense pogroms in Russia.

**1897** First Zionist Congress in Basel inspired by Theodor Herzl's vision of a Jewish state. The Congress agrees on the "Foundation of a legal homeland for the Jewish people in Palestine" but also discusses territorial alternatives, such as Uganda and Argentina.

**1905** The Seventh Zionist Congress finally agrees on Palestine as the future homeland of the Jewish people.

**1917** Great Britain seizes Palestine from Turkey. The efforts of Zionist leader Chaim Weizmann prompt the British Foreign Minister Lord Balfour to state in a letter: "Her Majesty regards the foundation of a national homeland for the Jewish people in Palestine benevolently." Chaim Weizmann later becomes the first president of the state of Israel.

**1936** Arab rebellion begins: first directed against Jewish civilians, later against the British authorities.

**1939** Beginning of World War II. Persecution of Jewish people all across Europe in the Holocaust. Great Britain promises the "Foundation of an independent Arab state in Palestine." Jewish immigration is drastically reduced. Jewish and Arab underground movements fight the British authorities.

**1947** The United Nations agrees on the partition of Palestine into a Jewish and an Arab state (map 1). Arab states reject this plan.

The Jewish population in Palestine rises from 24,000 to 630,000 due to several waves of immigration (*aliyah*; plural, *aliyot*) between 1882 and 1948. This more than triples Palestine's Jewish population at that time.

**1948** Declaration of the independent state of Israel on May 14 by Israel's first prime minister, David Ben-Gurion. On the following day, troops from Egypt, Jordan, Iraq, Syria, Lebanon, and Saudi Arabia attack Israel. The Jewish underground movements, *Lechi* and *Ezel*, launch a wave of attacks against Arab civilians, which culminates in the massacre at Deir Yassin, where 245 inhabitants lost their lives. According to UN estimates, 700,000 Palestinians fled or were driven out of their homes.

**1949** After the armistice, Israel alters the borders to its advantage (map 2). The West Bank has been annexed by Jordan; the Gaza Strip has been occupied by Egypt. UN resolution 194 guarantees the "right to return or compensation" to Palestinian refugees. Israel rejects the resolution because the refugees "had left their homes of their own free

**UN Partition Plan of 1947**

▪▪▪▪ Border of the British mandate
for Palestine 1922–1947

▨ The proposed Jewish state

▨ The proposed Arab state

▥ Jerusalem and its suburbs
designated as an international area

LEBANON

○ Sur

SYRIA

Akko ○

Haifa ○

*Sea of Galilee
(Lake Kinneret)*

○ Nazareth

○ Irbid

Jenin ○

*Jordan River*

Nablus ○

Jaffa ○ ○ Tel Aviv

Ramallah ○

○ Jericho    ○ Amman

*Mediterranean
Sea*

Jerusalem

Bethlehem ○

*Dead
Sea*

○ Gaza

Hebron ○

Beersheba ○

**ISRAEL**

*Negev
Desert*

**JORDAN**

*Sinai*

**EGYPT**

○ Maan

0  20  40  60  80  100 km

Eilat ○
○ Akaba

Map 1

will." Most Arab states, with the exception of Jordan, refuse to integrate the refugees into their populations. According to the UN, there are still 1.3 million Palestinians living in refugee camps in the West Bank, Gaza, Syria, and Lebanon. The estimated 1.5 million Palestinians living within the borders of Israel (except the West Bank, Gaza, and East Jerusalem) are now Israeli citizens.

**1964** The Arab League (parent organization of the Arab states)founds the Palestine Liberation Organization (PLO), whose goal is to "free all of Palestine."

**1967** Egyptian President Gamal Abdel Nasser mobilizes his army and closes down Israeli access to the Gulf of Akaba. On June 5, Israel attacks Egypt in a preemptive strike. Syria and Jordan declare war on Israel. After six days, the Israeli army captures the Sinai Peninsula and the Gaza Strip from Egypt, the Golan Heights from Syria, the West Bank and East Jerusalem (with the Old City) from Jordan (map 3). The United Nations passes resolution 242, which demands that Israel "retreat from Occupied Areas and that Arab states officially recognize Israel as a state and guarantees its borders."

**1967–1969** Yassir Arafat's extremist organization Al Fatah (Arabic for "conquest") takes the leading role within the PLO. Its strategy is armed combat with Israel. The Israeli government founds settlements in strategic positions in the West Bank, mainly the Jordan valley.

**1973** Egypt and Syria attack Israel on the Day of Atonement, Yom Kippur. The U.S. mediates an armistice. The

Boundaries of Israel 1949–1967

Territory of Israel as suggested by the UN Partition Plan. However the Arabs would never accept the plan

Territory outside the UN boundaries, that were occupied by Israel 1948–1949

West Jordan, occupied by Jordan

Gaza Strip, occupied by Egypt

LEBANON

Saida

Damascus

Sur

SYRIA

Akko

Sea of Galilee (Lake Kinneret)

Haifa

Nazareth

Irbid

Mediterranean Sea

Jenin

Nablus

Jordan River

Tel Aviv

Jaffa

Ramallah

Jericho

Amman

Jerusalem

Bethlehem

Gaza

Hebron

Dead Sea

Beersheba

ISRAEL

Sinai

Negev Desert

JORDAN

EGYPT

Maan

Eilat

Akaba

0  20  40  60  80  100 km

Map 2

Map 3

UN Security Council passes resolution 338, which calls upon both parties to forge a just and permanent peace. The PLO rejects resolutions 242 and 338 and garners international attention through hijackings and acts of terrorism against Jewish and Israeli civilians.

**1977** Menachem Begin, head of the ultraconservative party Likud, wins the elections in Israel and becomes prime minister. He pushes to found more settlements in occupied areas. To date, there have been a total of 145 settlements founded (map 4).

Egypt's President Anwar Sadat announces his willingness to enter into direct peace negotiations with Israel. In his speech at the Israeli parliament, he is the first Arab leader to acknowledge the legal existence of Israel.

**1979** Israel and Egypt sign the peace treaty of Camp David, which was mediated by U.S. President Jimmy Carter. Israel agrees to give back the Sinai Peninsula, from which it withdraws completely in 1981.

**1982** Because of the constant attacks by PLO guerrillas in northern Israel, the government, under Begin, agrees on operation Peace for Galilee. The goal is to create a 40-kilometer-wide security zone in southern Lebanon. But the Israeli army, under commander Ariel Sharon, reaches out as far as the Lebanese capital, Beirut. In September, Christian-Lebanese militias commit a massacre in the Palestinian refugee camps of Sabra and Shatilla. Over three hundred are killed and almost one thousand are missing. An Israeli investigating committee finds Ariel Sharon indirectly guilty. He

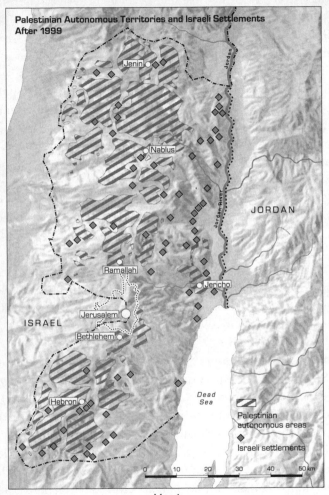

Palestinian Autonomous Territories and Israeli Settlements After 1999

Jenin

Nablus

JORDAN

Ramallah

Jericho

ISRAEL

Jerusalem

Bethlehem

Dead Sea

Hebron

Palestinian autonomous areas

Israeli settlements

0 10 20 30 40 50 km

Map 4

is forced to resign and is dismissed from the position of the Minister of Defense.

**1987** Beginning of the Intifida (literally, "to shake off"), the rebellion of mainly young Palestinians against the Israeli occupation. Israel reacts with "zero tolerance." In the first year of the Intifada, 450 Palestinians and 11 Israelis are killed. In opposition to the nationalistic PLO, Israel supports the foundation of Islamic factions, which will be the origin of the fundamentalist Hamas (Arabic for "enthusiasm/excitement") under its leader Sheikh Achmed Yassin.

**1988** PLO leader Yassir Arafat acknowledges UN resolutions 242 and 338 and thus the legal status of Israel. Furthermore, he condemns terrorism and commits himself to a peaceful solution to the conflict through negotiations.

**1990** The Iraqi president Saddam Hussein invades Kuwait. He refuses to retreat from Kuwait despite strict demands by the UN. Yassir Arafat's PLO supports Saddam Hussein.

**1991** An international alliance under the leadership of the U.S., and with the participation of almost all Arab states, frees Kuwait from Iraqi troops. Palestinians living in Kuwait and the Gulf region are expelled. The PLO loses its financial support throughout the Gulf region and Saudi Arabia.

Under pressure from George H.W. Bush, peace talks between Israel and a Jordanian-Palestinian delegation take place in Madrid. Simultaneously, the Israeli government enforces the extension of settlements in the West Bank. Hamas activists try to end the negotiations through terrorist acts.

**1992** The Labor party, under Itchzak Rabin and Shimon Peres, wins the elections in Israel. The party prohibits the foundation of new settlements. In Oslo, secret negotiations start with key representatives of the PLO.

**1993** The negotiations in Oslo result in a "Declaration of Principles," which is signed in September in Washington. Israel should retreat little by little from occupied areas and an autonomous Palestinian government should take over their administration. Within five years, final negotiations should make decisions about the most difficult questions, such as settlements, water, borders, and the status of Jerusalem.

**1994** Yassir Arafat returns from Tunis to Gaza after spending his whole life in exile. From 1994 through mid-1995, the Israeli army retreats from parts of Gaza and all Palestinian cities in the West Bank (zone A). In other areas (zone B), Palestinians become partly autonomous (map 4). Hamas commits suicide bombings with the goal of sabotaging the peace process. For Hamas, Palestine in its entirely is holy Islamic land to which Israel has no claim.

**1995** On November 4, a right-wing extremist assassinates Israeli Prime Minister Itzchak Rabin, believing that the "holy Jewish land" will not be returned to the Palestinian "enemies."

**1996** First elections for a Palestinian parliament. Yassir Arafat is confirmed as president. After a series of terrorist acts by Hamas, Benjamin Netanyahu, the leader of the conservative Likud, wins the elections in Israel. He dramatically slows down the negotiations by insisting that Palestinian President Yassir Arafat would first make a "hundred percent effort" to fight terrorism.

**1999** Ehud Barak of the Labor party becomes the new Israeli prime minister. He immediately strives for renewed negotiations.

**2000** Summit conference between Arafat and Barak at Camp David in the U.S. Despite intensive efforts by U.S. President Bill Clinton, the negotiations fail. An official record of the negotiations is never published. Since the beginning of the peace process in Oslo, the number of Jewish settlers in the West Bank and Gaza has doubled, to almost two hundred thousand. On September 29, Ariel Sharon, leader of the Israeli opposition, visits Haram Al-Sharif (holy to Islam), the Temple Mount (holy to Judaism) in Jerusalem. Several people are killed by the Israeli army during Palestinian protests the next day. Beginning of the Al-Aqsa Intifada. Marwan Barghouthy, a Palestinian representative from Ramallah and until then a strict supporter of peaceful solutions, organizes and becomes the leader of the Fatah affiliated *Tanzim*, the armed resistance against Israeli authorities. During negotiations in the Egyptian resort of Taba, U.S. President Bill Clinton suggests the "Clinton Parameters": Israel and Palestine would share Jerusalem as their capital. Israel must retreat from 95% of the West Bank. Israel accepts; PLO Chairman Yassir Arafat rejects the Clinton Parameters. The Palestinian delegation insists on the principle of the right of all Palestinian refugees to return to their homeland within Israel.

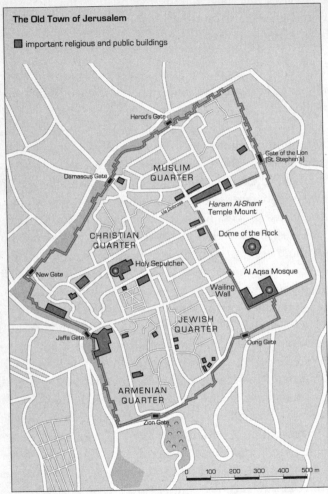

**The Old Town of Jerusalem**

■ important religious and public buildings

Herod's Gate

Gate of the Lion
(St. Stephen's)

Damascus Gate

MUSLIM
QUARTER

Via Dolorosa

*Haram Al-Sharif*
Temple Mount

Dome of the Rock

CHRISTIAN
QUARTER

New Gate

Holy Sepulcher

Al Aqsa Mosque

Wailing
Wall

Jaffa Gate

JEWISH
QUARTER

Dung Gate

ARMENIAN
QUARTER

Zion Gate

0   100   200   300   400   500 m

Map 5

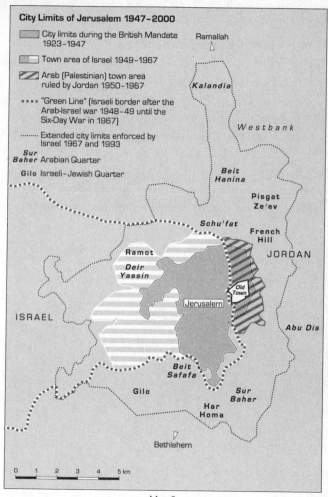

**City Limits of Jerusalem 1947–2000**

City limits during the British Mandate 1923–1947

Town area of Israel 1949–1967

Arab (Palestinian) town area ruled by Jordan 1950–1967

"Green Line" (Israeli border after the Arab-Israel war 1948–49 until the Six-Day War in 1967)

Extended city limits enforced by Israel 1967 and 1993

*Sur Baher* Arabian Quarter

*Gilo* Israeli–Jewish Quarter

Ramallah

*Kalandia*

*Westbank*

*Beit Hanina*

Pisgat Ze'ev

*Schu'fat*

French Hill

Ramot

*Deir Yassin*

JORDAN

Old Town

Jerusalem

ISRAEL

Abu Dis

*Beit Safafa*

Gilo

*Sur Baher*

Har Homa

Bethlehem

0  1  2  3  4  5 km

Map 6

Israel understands this as a complete destruction of the Israeli state through demographic measures.

**2001** After early elections in Israel, Ariel Sharon leader of the ultraconservative Likud party, becomes the new prime minister of Israel.

**2003** Ariel Sharon again re-elected as prime minister of Israel. Palestinian President Yassir Arafat appoints moderate Machmud Abbas, a.k.a. Abu Mazen, as prime minister. Both Ariel Sharon and Machmud Abbas agree to negotiate on a "road map to peace," designed by the so-called "quartet"—the United States, the United Nations, Russia, and the European Union.

# GLOSSARY

*Aliyah* (plural, *Aliyot*; Hebrew for "going up"): Immigration of Jews to Israel.

*Al-Kuds*: Arabic word for "The Holy," Arabic name for Jerusalem.

Allah: Arabic derivative of *Al llha,* God. One's devotion to Allah, the only God, and Mohammed, His prophet, is the first of the "five pillars" (dogmas) of Islam.

Friday prayer: The most important prayer of the Muslim week, which is accompanied with sermons by the mosque's first preacher.

Haram Al-Sharif or the Temple Mount in Jerusalem: According to the Bible (2 *Chronicles* 3.1) "King Solomon began building the temple on Mount Moriah in Jerusalem." This is where Abraham readied himself to sacrifice his only son (named Isaac according to the Hebrew Bible and Ishmael according to the Koran). In 586 B.C., the Babylonians destroyed the First Temple. It was rebuilt seventy years later and lavishly enlarged by King Herod. The Romans destroyed the Second Temple in A.D. 70 and drove out the greater part of Jerusalem's Jewish population. The reconstruction of the Temple was allowed by neither the Romans nor by the succeeding Byzantine sovereigns. From the Temple of the Herodian era, only the outer western wall remained. Since then, the Jewish people have bemoaned the razing of their Temple (the Wailing Wall is all that remains). Caliph Omar ibn al Khatib, who conquered Jerusalem in A.D. 638, ordered the building of a prayer-house. At the end of the seventh century, his successor built the Dome of the Rock and the Al-Aqsa Mosque. According to the Koran, Haram Al-Sharif is the place where the prophet Mohammad, accompanied by the angel Gabriel, started his nightly journey to God's throne (sura al Isra 17). According to the Jewish tradition, the Third Temple will be built there after the Coming of the Messiah.

Haggada (Hebrew word for "narration/story"—see Seder)

*Id al-Fitr*: The last day of Ramadan, the Islamic month of fasting.

*Leilat al-Kadr*: The night of the 26TH to the 27TH day of Ramadan. According to Islam, the angel Gabriel descends from heaven to earth that night and prays for the blessing of humankind.

Masada: Mountain fortress on the shore of the Dead Sea, where almost one thousand Jewish rebels barricaded themselves against the Roman occupying power. In A.D. 73 they committed mass suicide to escape Roman capture.

Mount Zion: Hill in the southeastern part of old Jerusalem, where the tomb of the biblical King David is believed to be.

Orthodox Jews (from Greek, to have the right belief/faith): Strictly religious Jews, who stringently follow all religious laws of Judaism.

Palestine (in Arabic *Falastin*): In A.D. 135, after the last Jewish rebellion against the Romans, the Emperor Hadrian renamed the province Judea "Palestina."

Purim: Jewish carnival holiday commemorating the Jews' triumph over the Persians.

Pesach: Jewish holiday to commemorate the departure of the Jewish people from Egypt (*Exodus*: 12–13).

Ramadan: The ninth month, according to the Islamic lunar calendar. It is celebrated with fasting from sunrise to sunset. It is believed that on this night, Muhammad first received the revelation of the Holy Koran.

Shabbat: The seventh day of the Jewish week. It starts on Friday evening and ends the next evening. This is a strict day of rest for orthodox Jews.

Seder (Hebrew for "order"): A celebration on the first evening of Pesach at which the narration (Haggada) of the departure of the Jewish slaves from Egypt is read.

Sukkot (Feast of Tabernacles): This is the Jewish Thanksgiving. The ancestral Israelites are remembered by building huts out of green twigs.

Tisha b' Av: The ninth day of the Jewish month of Av, which commemorates the destruction of the First and the Second Temples.

Temple Mount (see Haram Al-Sharif)

Wailing Wall (see Haram Al-Sharif or Temple Mount)

Yom Kippur (Day of Atonement): The holiest day in Judaism, which is celebrated with strict fasting. According to the Bible, the high priest asks for forgiveness for all the sins of the people of Israel.

Zionism: The origins of this Jewish national movement go back to the end of the nineteenth century in Europe. Its goal was the return of all Jews to the land of Israel, *Eretz Israel,* and to Jerusalem (according to the Bible, also named Zion).

## ACKNOWLEDGMENTS

I would like to thank Alicia Brooks, my editor at St. Martin's Press; Sally Richardson, publisher of St. Martin's Press; Matthew Shear, senior V.P. publisher of the Griffin imprint; Julia Kühn, my editor at Rowohlt Berlin, and Siv Bublitz, publisher of Rowohlt Berlin, for their thorough editing and insightful feedback. My thanks are also owed to my agent, Ariane Fink, at Sanford Greenburger, and the publicity team led by the dynamic publicity manager John Karle, whose peerless efforts and excellent teamwork have made it possible for this book to reach a wide readership.

—Sylke Tempel